the final dance

What The Dying Teach Us About
... EMBRACING LIFE

To Jane,

May you experience the
Joy that you give to others.

Cheryl

CHERYL DEINES, MSW

Editors:
Dale Metcalfe
Maureen Rafael

Cover & Interior Design:
Patricia D'Arrigo

Interior Design & Formatting:
Streetlight Graphics

ISBN-13: 978-1-7321400-0-4
ISBN-10: 1732140006
Printed in the United States of America

Author's Note

The descriptions in *The Final Dance* do not identify individuals. At the very heart of social work is the precept of confidentiality, and I have taken painstaking measures to insure the privacy of all real persons. All names are fictitious and all other recognizable features have been changed.

The people, events, and conversations presented here are taken from my seventeen years of work with hospice. However, because of my commitment to confidentiality, the people and circumstances portrayed in these pages are composite in nature; that is to say, each case represents a great many individuals whose characteristics and experiences have been adapted conceptually, carefully altered in their specifics, and combined to form an illustrative character. Any resemblance of such a composite character to any actual person is entirely coincidental. The experiences I share are universal. If a real name is used, it is with permission of the individual or is publicly-known information.

Table of Contents

The Taboo Of Death

Orienting to Death

Dancing With Death

My Expansion

Final Thoughts

Healing Exercises

The Final Dance is dedicated to the courageous souls I have been privileged to walk with through the last days of their lives and their beloved family members who bravely faced life without their loved ones. Thank you for allowing me to companion you through your sacred journeys. You have been my greatest teachers.

Author's Preface

I HAD NEVER INTENDED TO WORK with the dying. Frankly, I was uncomfortable with the whole idea of being with someone who was at the end of life. And I couldn't imagine having to talk to people who were terminally ill about their impending death or having to counsel family members about their loved one's terminal illness. Believe me, I did not seek out hospice work. But it sure did find me.

It found me through an unpredictable series of events that took place around the critical illness of my younger sister Shelly. With hindsight I can see how synchronistic those events proved to be for my life. I have since come to believe that there are no accidents.

Just as I was hesitant to work with the dying, I was also reluctant to write this book for several reasons. First, I came to feel extremely protective of my patients, their stories, and their bereaved family members. Although I knew that I could always change their names and identifying information to protect their privacy (which I have done), I also felt a tremendous responsibility to handle their stories with the utmost care. Because I know firsthand what a privilege it is to be with my hospice patients and their families during these precious and tender moments, I did not want to take that privilege lightly nor diminish it in any way.

Second, I was concerned that writing these stories might result in my spending the rest of my career being asked to speak professionally about death and dying from a limited clinical perspective. To be honest with you, that felt like a heavy sentence–especially since my work in hospice has connected me more and more deeply with my own joy in living. Ironic as it might sound, it is my work in hospice as a counselor to the dying and the grieving that has tapped me into my true passion: living life to its fullest.

I felt other resistances to writing this book as well. Not the least of these was taking on the task of writing a book—much less a book about a topic as sensitive as death and dying. But in spite of them all there was an undeniable stirring within me, and it simply refused to budge. As hard as I tried I couldn't shake it, quell it, or talk it into focusing on something else. As the weeks and months passed it eased its way from the background into the foreground of my consciousness, until the day that I simply had to give in and say yes.

I said yes in much the same way that you may have said yes when you chose to read this book. That yes is a letting go of resistance . . . a leap of faith . . . a nod to stepping off a safe but ill-defined edge that's just always been there . . . and a choosing to begin the exploration of what's beyond that edge.

My intention in writing this book is to share deeper aspects of the human end-of-life experience. Why? Because these aspects are both precious and profound. They have the power to enhance our everyday lives in untold ways. I believe that, because we live in a culture that shies away from facing death, we routinely and unconsciously make the mistake of impoverishing our own lives.

My desire is that *The Final Dance* enriches the lives of all who read it, just as my patients have so immeasurably enriched mine. In it I retell some of the meaningful stories that were entrusted to me, and I address important questions about dying. I also share my patients' beautiful and poignant insights into life. It is my sincere hope that you will receive these stories and lessons as the profound messages for "living life" that they are. These beautiful gifts that I have been privileged to receive are what I share with you. I invite you to open them for yourself. As you do so, you may be surprised and delighted by what you find.

Yes, it's true that many of my hospice patients die, but death itself is not the primary focus of our time together. Our focus is on sharing the narrative of their lives. In *The Final Dance* you will hear what I have heard: what makes a good life, the blessings of affection and humor, and the importance of appreciating the simple joys in everyday life that we so often don't have time for, take for granted, or just overlook.

There is no doubt in my mind that the wisdom I have received from my patients as they lay dying have been the source of my personal liberation. *The Final Dance* is the best way I know how to share the heart and soul of what I have learned with you, story by story. With this book in hand you are now invited to be the mindful witness and to receive the gifts that await you. May they serve to liberate you, opening you to choose for yourself the largest, most joyful life imaginable.

How To Use This Book

THE FINAL DANCE IS ARRANGED in six sections. After each chapter, I offer a series of "questions to dance with" which will support you in your own exploration into your beliefs, how you live your life, and what you can do to enhance or improve your life.

The first section (*The Taboo of Death*), looks at where the entire discussion of death and dying fits— or more precisely, doesn't fit— into our cultural mores. We take a look at how the media's portrayal of death keeps us dancing around the subject of death with our backs to it, thus making it nearly impossible for us to really see life as it is or to wholeheartedly engage in it. I discuss how turning to face your death can benefit you and your life.

The second section (*Orienting to Death*), gives an eagles-eye view of my personal journey, which brought me, most unexpectedly, to my hospice career. I share this part of my life so that you have a better understanding of how hospice work has impacted the way I view life and, consequently, the way I have come to live my own.

The third section *(Dancing with Death),* includes stories of the most poignant personal experiences I have had with hospice patients. In sharing these stories my hope is that you will gain powerful insights from them, insights that may prompt you to take a closer look at your own life. After each of these stories I share the personal lesson (found in the highlighted sections) I learned from the experience as I worked with these incredible souls. Each lesson is followed by questions to give you an opportunity to explore more deeply how these lessons might apply to your life.

In the fourth section (*My Expansion*), I share how my life has been impacted as a result of my work with the dying. I explore how it has been enhanced and changed thanks to the generous insights my patients have shared and the lessons they have learned (or wish they had learned) as they journeyed through life.

Section five (*Final Thoughts*), explores how our modern society has become so disconnected from life, death, and each other, examining how this disconnection can impact our lives and relationships. There are also some suggestions on how to be with another when they are facing death and how this way of being can benefit all areas of your life.

In section six (*Healing Exercises*), I offer several exercises to support you in deepening your explorations of the issues at hand. They include guided visualizations, journaling prompts, and other creative exercises.

Many of you may find that you welcome the explorations in this book and that you would like to go even further with them. With this in mind, I have created a companion workbook (*The Final Dance Workbook*) which can be used along with this book to take your personal exploration even deeper. The workbook, along with downloadable recordings of the visualizations, are available on amazon.com and my website (www.cheryldeines.com).

Introduction

I HAD LOST MY BELIEF IN mankind after ten years of working as a
social worker with victims of child abuse and witnessing the dark
side of humanity on a daily basis. My zest for life was gone. I was
demoralized, burnt-out, and merely surviving. I lived for the weekends,
and I had taken to numbing myself out with alcohol to dull the images of
violence that I was exposed to throughout the week. I longed to be rescued
from my sad and disheartened life. Then, starting in 1998, I experienced
a series of events (including illness, death and an existential crisis) that
made me take a good hard look at the way I was living my life. As a result,
I chose to make changes that drastically improved my life.

When I began to work for hospice that process was accelerated. My
experiences with hospice patients became guideposts for how to see my
life more clearly, make real life changes and truly engage in life more
fully. Each patient I encountered offered me a special lesson about living.
As I began to apply those lessons to my own life, I reconnected with
myself once again. My true passion for living was rekindled.

This book is your invitation to learn what I have learned from the dying.
By sharing the courage hospice patients model in the face of their own

impending deaths, you will meet courage in a new way. Their courage has inspired me to live more boldly; you, too, may find the inspiration to take risks, to allow yourself to be more vulnerable and authentic, and to speak from your heart.

Just as the inspiration and soulful gifts given to me by my hospice patients have enabled me to reconnect with my joy in life and my love for people, you, too, will encounter these opportunities. The perceptions shared by these patients may well give you just the right nudges to open yourself to new ways of being "you" in the world—more loving, more forgiving, more joyfully connected.

In our culture, how often are we encouraged to take—or make—the opportunity to turn and face our own death? Rarely. Most of us don't have any idea what that would even begin to look like. But as I have been blessed, over and over again, to companion others through their transition, it has given me a whole new perspective on what is truly important in life. Step by step, I share how that process has unfolded for me. Step by step, you will be inspired to live your life more fully, to wake up to aspects of life that have been passing you by.

You will see how acknowledging the temporary nature of life or a terminal diagnosis gives people an opportunity to take care of unfinished business. Hospice professionals often help patients explore whether there are things they had hoped to accomplish in life that are still possible for them to do. They then enlist the help of their family members to make it happen. This kind of involvement of family members is often what finally enables *the breakthrough of the death taboo* to happen. Its repercussions can be family-wide, healing and profound.

One example of this occurred when my team members worked with a woman who was a quadriplegic who often talked about her love of swimming, how much she missed it, and how much she wished that she could swim one last time. Arrangements were made for her to be taken to a private pool by ambulance, then a Hoyer lift was provided to lower her into the pool. Staff and family were present to assist her. She had a look of ecstasy as she was gently lowered into the warm salt water. We were thrilled to be able to provide her with the opportunity for one last "swim."

Many times our patients' wishes are as easily fulfilled as that one, but not always. When a patient's unfulfilled dreams are much bigger and not as easily simulated, I've often felt powerless to do anything but help them come to terms with an unfulfilled life. The goal becomes helping them get to a place of acceptance about their impending death and to a positive place where they can anchor themselves beyond their regrets.

It was the feelings of powerlessness that motivated me to write this book. Although I couldn't help my patients go for their big dreams (their time had run out), I knew that sharing their stories might light a fire under others to go for theirs. I felt a sense of urgency, wanting to throw my windows open and call out to all who could hear me, "Wake up!! *This* is your life. No more waiting for the right time! No more excuses!" Instead, I write, hoping that these stories will fall into the hands of those who need them most. The knowledge I share here is what helped me to wake up to my life.

I have seen the same core issues come up for patient after patient. A majority of these were pure and simple regrets: about chances not taken, about not allowing others to see them for who they were, about not finding their true purpose in life, and regrets about "sleep walking" through their lives. Importantly, their regrets were usually not about what they had done. Rather, they were about the risks they hadn't taken, the relationships they had not healed, the dreams they hadn't allowed themselves to dream.

Over and over again, I've heard patients in the last days of their lives say, "I thought I had more time." They were truly disappointed that they had waited "for a more convenient time" to travel, to write, to relax. They deeply regretted "playing it safe in life" and felt like they had missed their opportunities to have a richer, fuller life. I heard the message loud and clear. Don't wait, *Do it NOW!* This was one of the first and most important lessons I learned from my patients.

One of my biggest and boldest accomplishments happened when I incorporated the *Do it NOW!* lesson into my own life. I took a trip around the world (on a social worker's income, no less!) Before I learned the *Do it NOW!* lesson, traveling around the world was a dream I never would have thought possible, much less put on my bucket list. But when that desire stirred within me, I went for it. In spite of the many well-meaning efforts of others to discourage or dissuade me from taking the trip, I knew that I shouldn't wait until "a more convenient time," until I had "more money," or until "my child was out of the house" (for me that was my dog).

As you will soon discover, *The Final Dance* is a book that will summon you to want to live "full out"—to have a richer life, to experience more joy, and to feel more fulfilled. As you read these stories you will feel inspired to reach for your dreams like never before. As you listen to these stories, allow them to touch you, to percolate down into your heart and inspire you to go after your dreams. *Do it NOW!*

It takes courage to go on a journey of self-exploration, especially one that opens your eyes over and over again to the taboo subject of death. I feel honored that you have selected *The Final Dance* to support you on your path of discovery. My wish for you is that you are gifted as I have been by the stories I share here. May these foundational and heartfelt life lessons from the dying transform your life as brilliantly as they have mine.

Cheryl Deines

The Taboo Of Death

Demystifying Death

Only when you accept that one day you'll die can you make the
best out of life. And that's the big secret. That's the Miracle.

~ Gabriel Ba ~

THIS BOOK COMES AT AN important time in our history. So
many of us in Western culture have been sheltered from the
experience of dying and death, and even from the very notion of
death being our own ultimate personal reality. For many decades of our
lives, death has been depicted with fear, violence and horror in television,
movies, and even comic books. And that ante keeps going nowhere but up,
especially in special effects. Gruesome images of death have proliferated
onto the internet, into video games and through social media.

All these media have cultivated a serious flirtation with "the dark side."
Relentlessly, they dramatize death with distorted images of pain and gore,
riveting suspense, horror, and unnatural death-dealing creatures of every
description. They have turned death into something to be feared, while
they persistently steer their imagery away from the true human experience
of death and dying, away from reality of death as the normal and natural
part of life that it is.

Sadly, for far too many of us, the media's images of death are the only ones we have any real exposure to until we are around middle age. Being neither true-to-life nor instructive in their portrayal of dying and death, these images must surely be influencing us, whether we realize it or not. My own experience leads me to believe that that influence is not beneficial. I have rarely seen a death portrayed on TV or in movies that looks like the real-life experiences that occur in hospice every day. I assume this is because the peaceful, quiet way most people die is neither riveting nor newsworthy.

And I would go one step further to say that the images of death that we are constantly being fed by visual media are perhaps more damaging, more invasive and more "anti-educational" than we realize. Precisely because Western culture–and most especially in the U.S.–has pushed death out beyond the bounds of general education, polite conversation, and easy acceptance. In other words, we have dropped the *real story* of dying and death out of what we learn about, out of the personal stories we are comfortable telling, and out of our lives' comfort zones.

As our society has "evolved" in this modern era, we have been so shielded from death that our treatment of the dying has become cold and distant. It used to be that several generations of a family lived in the same household and most deaths happened at home. The family members all knew when one of their own was dying. They nursed one another through their illnesses and gathered around when one of them was dying. Today it is a much different story.

Our families tend to be spread out all over the country, sometimes even the world. It is far more common today for our elders to be placed in nursing homes, hospice houses or hospitals, than allowed to die at home, surrounded and supported by their families. After the death, their loved one's body is discretely removed, the family often choosing not to view them.

As a result of these new cultural mores and the lack of close experience that the average person has with relatives who are aging and dying, family members are often uncomfortable (even terrified) of witnessing the end of a loved one's life. Believe me when I say that there is no condemnation coming from me about the wide-ranging emotionality around experiencing death. I know these fears well. Not wanting to be there when the patient takes their last breath. Not wanting to view the body. Not wanting to deal with the flood of others' emotions. Not wanting to acknowledge others' emotions, much less begin to own and process one's own. I know these fears because I experienced all of them firsthand when I started working in hospice.

As a hospice social worker, I understand how utterly unprepared for death we can be. I have worked with many people who have gone numb in the face of the death of a loved one. I have counseled individuals who felt overwhelmed by grief, individuals who were angered by grief, and others who dangerously repressed their grief. I have companioned people who are stunned by death, those who are affronted by it, people who are panicked by it, and those who are in abject denial of it. I have seen people who are so unprepared for death that it is as if the very real possibility of death had never occurred to them.

I have come to see just how important it is to turn toward the end of our life and look squarely at it. We need to learn to accept the inevitability of death. Imagine how different our lives would be if we saw death for what it is, accepted it, and embraced it. Until we do, we will continue to cheat ourselves out of the very gifts that death offers us to illuminate the whole of our lives. These are the gift of clarity about what really matters, the gift of courage to follow our heart's calling, the gift of freedom to authentically speak our truth, and the gift of wisdom to let go of what holds us back.

We owe it to ourselves to feed our personal imaginations with images that see death as the natural, non-threatening phenomenon that it is. We could start by simply talking about death instead of avoiding that conversation at every turn as so many of us do. We can have conversations throughout our lives that enhance our understanding of what will happen to our loved ones in their dying process–and what will inevitably happen to each of us. Such honest communication will foster a healthy understanding of the role that death plays in all of our lives.

If our society were more comfortable with the topic of death and if there were open dialogue there would be less resistance to talking about death when someone is facing a terminal illness. My hope is that *The Final Dance* will support people in opening up to these important conversations years before they are actually facing death.

I have come to appreciate that my vantage point as a hospice professional is unique. I recently read an article on quora.com that said the average person who lives to be ninety experiences about fifty deaths in their lifetime. (About half of those deaths occur when they are seventy-five or older, by the way.) What I realized is that, unlike most people, I experience death on a regular basis. I've averaged 40-hour work weeks for the past seventeen years and often experience several deaths a week. Occasionally, I have experienced more than one death in the same day. I would say that I have easily experienced "a lifetime worth of deaths" each year that I have worked in hospice. I see how my experience sets me apart from most people in our culture.

I am also grateful that I have been gifted with both curiosity and an open mind. I entered hospice work with no agenda other than wanting to understand what my patients and their family members were experiencing. This approach enabled me, as a hospice social worker, to create a safe place for my patients to explore whatever they needed to explore at the end of their lives. As I counseled patients and their families, I have become aware that there is deep wisdom, an essential stream of truth, within each of us. It's this internal guidance that I often access as I am engaged with my patients in order to best serve them. Some of my most meaningful moments in life have been those in which I have been able to hold space for others to find the truth that wells up from within and the celebration of their arrival at that discovery. The great news is that this wisdom is not just reserved for our death bed but is accessible to us anytime!

Each of my patients has been precious and unique. Each has shared their very particular life story that is unlike anyone else's. I have been privileged to have deep and meaningful conversations with hospice patients as they face the end of their lives. They speak to me about their fears, regrets and joys, as well as the lessons they've learned along the way. They have often shared with me in a way that they didn't feel they could share with their own families. Through these interactions I became aware of a common thread that runs through many of their experiences.

I have come to recognize the beautiful patterns that seem to be imbedded in the dying process itself. I've noticed profound commonalities in what people are experiencing as they approach their death, what happens when they make their transition, and what happens after that.

My great hope in sharing these stories is that you, too, will see another way of being with your loved ones who are dying. And my hope is even bigger than that. . . .

As you continue to read this book I invite you to recognize that, underneath it all, this book is fundamentally about "a way of being." Yes, it is about a way of being that offers you and your dying family member true solace as you companion them and bring your full presence to their final dance. But even beyond that, the lessons shared in this book are really about "the whole enchilada" we call life. This way of being is yours to live and yours to give, *no matter the life circumstances* you are faced with.

Now here's the sweet lesson that I want to share with you and that I want you to learn from. Through my hospice experience I can honestly attest to a far different experience than the one that our culture has allowed us to build up such fears about. I have come to know that death— although messy at times, just as childbirth is— is a most beautiful and sacred time in our human experience. It is a truly precious time to be together, to be "with" another person.

I now consider it an honor to share the final dance with someone in their last weeks and days, and certainly at that moment that they draw their last breath. I understand if you are hesitant or uncomfortable with this topic. As I said, I certainly was uncomfortable prior to my hospice experiences. I now know what a gift the awareness of death is. It impacts the way I interact with my friends, my family, and the way I live my life.

It may be that you haven't thought much about death because it has not touched your life. Or maybe you had a traumatic experience around death at a young age that shut you down to questioning or further seeking. And because of this it may feel scary to look at death. But I assure you that there can be many treasures and gifts in this exploration.

Based on the extraordinary liberation into life that my time in hospice has given me, my fervent hope is that you will allow yourself to be as present as you can as you read the personal stories on the pages to come. I encourage you to acknowledge any fears and anxieties about death that may arise in you, and I urge you to give those feelings whatever space and attention they may need. Please know that the gift you give yourself by taking these stories to heart may be one of the greatest gifts you will ever receive.

Above all, I know that the awareness of the impermanence of this life can have far-reaching positive effects on how you live your life. I would encourage you to begin exploring your feelings about this tender topic through the journaling exercise and questions on the next page. Should you experience any momentary discomfort as you entertain these thoughts, know that on the other side of this discomfort, freedom awaits.

Journaling Exercise: I would encourage you to simply "sit" with your feelings about dying and write about what comes up for you. Are there questions, fears, feelings that come when you think about death? This activity will support you on getting clear on what you do believe, as well as identifying any questions you might have. I trust that many of those questions will be answered as you continue to read *The Final Dance*.

Questions to Dance With...

Do you ever allow yourself to think about dying? (If so, what are your thoughts?) (If not, why do you avoid this topic?)

What experiences have you had around death? How have those experiences impacted you?

What questions come up for you when you think about death?

Orienting to Death

Turning Toward Death

Sometimes what is in the way, is the way.

~ Mark Nepo ~

I FELT PANIC AS I SAT in an orientation class for new hospice employees, thinking, "Oh my God! I might have to talk to people about the fact that they are dying, or actually sit with someone as they die. What have I gotten myself into?" At that moment, I had no idea what an impact my hospice work would come to have on my life. Strangely enough, I never intended to get involved in hospice work. I now believe that I was led to this work.

My journey began earlier that year when my little sister Shelly became ill. Her body was rejecting the kidney she had received 16 years earlier from a 20-year-old stranger who died in a motorcycle accident. She was in need of another transplant. The doctors approached my family, asking if anyone would consider being tested as a possible donor. My entire family stepped forward willing to donate.

Neither of my parents were healthy enough to be considered. Two of my siblings were tested and told they couldn't donate due to their personal health risks. Initially, the doctors told me they wouldn't consider me due to a pre-existing health condition. By the time my siblings were ruled out we had watched my sister's weight drop from 105 to 79 pounds. We were watching her fade away before our eyes.

It had taken six months for her doctors to test my siblings, and I knew she didn't have another six months. I personally fought hospital policy, pushing for them to consider me as a potential donor. When they finally agreed to test me, I drove to the Mayo clinic in Rochester, Minnesota in order to expedite the testing, and went through a barrage of medical tests and procedures to prove that I was healthy enough to donate. There I immersed myself in the very medical world that I had spent most of my life avoiding, being tested, poked and prodded. After two months of testing it was determined that I was a perfect match for my sister and healthy enough to be her donor.

A few weeks later my left kidney was removed and placed in my sister Shelly's body. Though physically painful, it was one of the most incredible experiences of my life because I had been able to keep my little sister alive. I was deeply moved by the outpouring of love and support that came from friends and family.

During this magical time, I received an unexpected gift. It was due to my recuperation from the kidney donation that I ended up sitting in that hospice orientation class. My plan had originally been to do my social work internship as a school counselor. Because of the surgery, I needed to start a month late but the school system was rigid and couldn't allow a late start. Hospice was more flexible. So, I had the option of either doing my internship with hospice and being able to graduate on time or waiting until the next semester to finish up.

In all honesty, the thought of working with people who were dying made me feel anxious. I had spent the past nine years working in child protective services. It was heavy, depressing work, and that was my view of hospice. I wanted to do something lighter, more fun.

Although the thought of being with people at the end of their lives made me uncomfortable, my desire to graduate was stronger than my fear of working with the dying. So I pushed through my discomfort and signed up to do my internship with hospice.

It was six weeks after surgery that I found myself sitting in that orientation, my body still aching. It felt surreal to be a captive audience in that tiny classroom listening to hospice professionals talk about how to be with people at the end of their lives. For many months, my family had fought so hard against death, and I had risked my own life to ensure that my sister lived. Now I realized I was being asked to face death head on, without the possibility of reprieve. Even with the skills they were trying to teach me, was I ready? Could I handle it? I didn't know.

I believe my anxiety was partially due to the fact that I didn't have strong beliefs about what happens after we die. I grew up in a conservative Midwestern town in Nebraska. My family was not particularly religious, rarely attending church except on major holidays.

As a child I attended church with my best friend, Tina, whose uncle was the minister of a Pentecostal Church. For me it was pure entertainment. The congregants were quite expressive with their *Amens* and *Hallelujahs!* The minister's wife would speak rapidly in what sounded like gibberish, her eyes rolling back in her head as if possessed, later translating the messages that came through her. I was always fascinated with the organ player who cried through every service, never missing a note, as tears poured down her face and onto the organ keys. My favorite part of these colorful services was the music. People sang loudly and off key with joyous abandon as they joined their voices in song.

Throughout my childhood and into my late twenties I participated in religious services sporadically. With eight mouths to feed, my parents were focused on survival and not much thought was given to existential matters. When we did go to church it was often an experience of public shaming, as well-meaning congregants were quick to point out how long it had been since we had last attended. Then there was the discomfort of sitting through sermons about what wretches and sinners we all were. Shame seemed to be the primary message.

I would walk out of these services feeling torn down, sinful and confused.

In reality, my only sin was nothing more than the recent pinching of my sister in the back seat of our old Ford station wagon when she squeezed in too close to me. Every time we went to these services it took several days for their negative effects to wear off. Needless to say, I was thankful that this was not an activity my parents insisted upon on a regular basis. I had many friends who weren't so lucky.

It wasn't until my widowed uncle remarried a woman named Rosie that I had the experience of having religion forced on me. Rosie was an otherwise sweet woman who was convinced that her new family would burn in hell if she did not intervene. She had made saving souls her mission in life, devoting many years to missionary work on an Indian reservation in order to bring her form of God to the Apache Indians. When she married my uncle, she turned her focus on our family.

We would all listen politely as she proselytized. And, believe me, we did a lot of polite listening! Aunt Rosie would make attempts to convert us any time she saw an opportunity. A few days before I was to move out of my parents' home in order to attend college, she called me into the kitchen so she could "pray for my salvation." I had been raised to be polite to my elders, so I went along with it. As Aunt Rosie prayed fervently, my little brother Kevin, seeing my dilemma, kept peeking around the corner in order to taunt me. I was holding my breath, attempting not to laugh, as my well-intentioned aunt continued to pray.

She paused occasionally to ask, "Can you feel Jesus in your heart?" I wasn't at all sure what that felt like but finally, out of desperation, I proclaimed, "Yes, I feel it!" in order to be set free from her urgent prayers. Being the rebel that I was, this was definitely not the way to introduce God to me! The more my aunt attempted to push God into my heart, the more I pushed back. It was many years before I set foot in a church again.

After graduating with my bachelor's degree in social work, I spent five years working in Nebraska with Child Protective Services investigating child abuse. During that time I saw the worst of humanity, witnessing the results of many horrible situations involving battered children. I felt burnt out and utterly disheartened with mankind. Not long after I had started my work in hospice someone asked me if it wasn't "really hard work to do." I told them that I felt death was a natural part of life and that it didn't feel "hard" because it was inevitable that people would die. I went on to say, "Now, Child Protective Service work . . . *that* was hard." Indeed, death is natural. But child abuse is the epitome of unnatural. To work with innocent children who had been beaten or raped was one of the most difficult things I have ever done.

After five years of investigating child abuse, I transferred into the foster care office, where I licensed and trained foster parents. I made the decision to transfer after a particularly gruesome day-long investigation. At the end of that day, I realized that although I had been with a little five-year-old girl who had been brutally beaten, I felt nothing. Immediately, I knew it was time for me to leave that job. I realized that I had arrived at the very place we had been warned about during our training in social work. I had begun to shut down my emotions in order to deal with the horrible things I was witnessing on a regular basis.

I am profoundly grateful that my training in social work emphasized the importance of being aware of our own emotional states and being able to identify when we reach the limit of our personal stress thresholds. When I moved over into foster care I experienced some immediate emotional relief, along with the return of some of my zest for helping make a difference in others' lives. It was there that I experienced a series of events that changed the direction of my life. I had been feeling restless, knowing deep inside that there was more to life than what I had been experiencing.

Around this time my co-worker Stephanie's twenty-eight-year-old husband Adam was killed in a car accident. I had attended their wedding a couple of years before, and Stephanie and I had grown close while working together. I didn't know Adam well, but his death deeply impacted me.

Soon after he died, I was attending a mandatory team-building workshop. During one of the afternoon sessions, we were led in a guided visualization that took us to a scene where we were witnessing our own funerals. We were guided to imagine that, one by one, our friends, family members and co-workers stood up and shared how we had impacted them and what we had accomplished in our lives.

To my own surprise, I wept through the entire visualization. I realized in those moments that I had been living without passion, direction or purpose. I had been merely "surviving." We were then asked to take an inventory of our lives. Through this exercise it became clear to me that if I were to die tomorrow, there would be many regrets and unfulfilled dreams left in the balance. I knew something had to change. And Adam's death had been a painful reminder that our lives could end at any moment. I left that workshop clear that there was much more I wanted to do with my life.

Although I was working in a career that many would call "noble" and "rewarding," I knew that my heart was no longer in it. I spent evenings and weekends at local bars with friends, numbing myself with alcohol, hoping to meet a knight in shining armor who would rescue me from my unfulfilled life. But there was no knight in sight.

I began looking at where I could make personal changes. I had been working on my master's degree and knew that graduating would be one accomplishment I would be proud of, as no one in my immediate family had ever attended college. As I sat thinking about what was next for me, I made two decisions: I decided to turn my attention towards school, and to start taking more risks.

During this time my friend Andrea kept trying to talk me into joining her at a spiritual retreat she was planning to attend. My initial response was, "I'm not going to spend a weekend with a bunch of holy rollers who are going to spew scripture at me and look down on me!" She laughed and assured me that it wasn't like that. Remembering my decision to take more risks, I finally changed my mind and agreed to attend.

I felt extremely awkward at the retreat at first. I realized I was uncomfortable relating to others in a social setting without a few beers under my belt. As I relaxed into the weekend, I experienced healing. It was a heart-opening experience for me, especially because I shared about my struggles with structured religion. To my surprise, others shared similar struggles. I discovered, much to my delight, that I wasn't so different after all.

One of my biggest *ahas* of the weekend was that even those who had always had a strong faith did not judge me for questioning. After having a positive experience at the retreat, I found myself opening to other group experiences. Soon after the retreat I joined a women's group that I had previously been hesitant to become involved with and began to create a healthy support system.

With the support of these loving women from all walks of life, I began to explore my own beliefs more deeply, to study different spiritual teachings, and to share my findings and observations. Because I did this in an environment of love and acceptance, I felt safe to continue to explore and to discover what felt true to me, even when it appeared to be at variance with more mainstream beliefs.

As part of my spiritual exploration I visited several different churches and spiritual centers. I was surprised to see how different their interpretations of the Bible were from denomination to denomination. During one Christian service, I was shocked when the minister made it clear that if you were gay or lesbian you were not welcome in their church. He actually asked people to leave. I was appalled by this and left the service, vowing never to set foot in that church again. Any church that excluded others was not a church I wanted to be a part of.

It was during this time of exploration that I donated my kidney to my younger sister. Something shifted at the very core of my being. It was subtle, yet profound. The feelings of unworthiness that I had carried for as long as I could remember faded away overnight. Donating my kidney was a big sacrifice. I had given of my body and my time, and I had done so without hesitation. There was something very powerful about giving so much to another human being.

I had been rebellious as a teenager and young adult, drinking and putting myself in dangerous situations. I continued to drink into my twenties and was ashamed of some of the things I had done during that time of heavy drinking. After donating my kidney to my sister, I felt like I had made up for some of the things I had done in my wilder days. Prior to the organ donation I had never attended a high school reunion because I believed that my classmates thought poorly of me. After donating my kidney, it was as if I had "proof" to offer to others that I was a good person. The reality was that my classmates were so caught up in their own experiences they really had not thought much about me.

I didn't know it at the time, but enduring the testing, the surgery and the recovery period for the kidney donation was also preparing me to work with the dying. After going to extremes to save my sister, I was better able to empathize with family members who weren't ready to give up or say goodbye to their loved ones in hospice. I also gained a glimpse into the kinds of experience that many of our patients go through prior to coming into hospice service. Their bodies had been traumatized— sometimes over a long period of time— by chronic and acute diseases, multiple tests, numerous medications, procedures and surgeries before they came on to hospice service. Having experienced some of those traumas firsthand, I had a deeper level of understanding and empathy for the patients under my care.

Initially, I had reservations about hospice, envisioning the work to be heavy and solemn. Although there were moments like that, I realized what a privilege it was to be with people during this sacred time in their lives. The true focus wasn't on dying but rather on "living"— how to find joy in the last days and moments of life, how to help people embrace their opportunities to examine their lives, how to support them to find ways to say goodbye to all they would leave behind, and, ultimately, what light they could shed on "how to live life" so that those who came after them might have the experience of feeling truly fulfilled at the end of life.

Within these next pages I have shared many intimate encounters that I've had with dying patients and their families. I have done my best to encourage you, my readers, to experience each of these sharing's as the precious gift it is. All you really need to know is that I've learned so much about "living" as I companioned these courageous souls through their final days and walked with their families through their journey of grief.

My hope for you is that you can open your heart to learning as I have learned. Allow yourself to be constantly reminded by these stories to live fully, love deeply, laugh often, and forgive. May the awareness of the impermanence and frailty of life remind you to embrace and step boldly into your own life.

Questions to Dance With...

We all have our personal stories and challenges that impact our feeling and beliefs about life. What have been some of those experiences in your life?

How have those experiences changed the way you view or live your life?

Have you had a time in your life that you would consider a "turning point" in your life? Describe it.

Dancing With Death

Going Home

A butterfly lights beside us like a sunbeam and for a brief moment
its glory and beauty belong to our world. But, then it flies on again,
and though we wish it could have stayed, we feel so lucky to have seen it.

~ Author Unknown ~

A FEW DAYS AFTER MY TWO-WEEK orientation ended, I was assigned one of my first patients. Eleanor was an eighty-year-old woman who was dying of end stage heart disease. She was a beautiful, dark-eyed, intelligent woman who exuded charm and elegance. In my training I had heard that people often die the way they've lived. I found this to be the case with Eleanor.

She was focused on taking care of business as she went through boxes of papers and pictures that she wanted to revisit and then destroy. Eleanor was widowed, had no children and no living relatives. She had no friends capable of doing this task when she was gone and being the private person she was, she did not want a stranger going through her things. Because she was growing weak this was not a task she could accomplish on her own, so the two of us began to sort through her boxes.

These boxes represented her life, a lifetime of memories, struggles, and joys. As we went through her old photos, I asked her what she wanted me to do with them and found it disturbing when she told me to throw them out. "They mean nothing to anyone but me." Coming from a large family, I couldn't imagine what it must feel like to be so alone in the world. As she shared the stories of her life, I realized that she was looking to me to keep her memory alive.

During the ten years I'd spent working with Child Protective Services, I had learned the importance of keeping clear boundaries and distance with clients. But something felt different about the relationship I was developing with Eleanor. I sensed the need to let my guard down in order to be with her fully.

She clearly didn't have time for a bunch of social-worker-psycho-babble. But even as I realized that she needed someone who was going to be real with her, I felt an internal struggle as I allowed myself to grow closer to her. Hoping I wasn't crossing the professional boundaries that had been drilled into my psyche as a social work student, instinctually, I knew that I served her more fully by allowing myself to connect with her, person to person. This didn't mean I shared personal information or burdened her with my issues, but I didn't pretend to have all the answers, and I allowed myself to love her. As I did so, it was clear that she felt safe with me. Eleanor was one of my first teachers. She taught me more about how to be with my patients than I had ever learned in my graduate studies.

While going through her boxes, she instructed me to read anything that looked important. If I felt it was something she would want to see, I was told to put it aside. Everything else she wanted shredded. It felt like a violation of privacy to read her papers, but with her encouragement I began to read through one after another, putting aside letters and more personal items that I felt Eleanor might want to look at one last time before she destroyed them. When she looked at what I had put aside, it often triggered a memory that she would share. I felt privileged be a part of her process as she reviewed her life.

As the sorting continued I ran across a letter written to Eleanor's now-deceased husband from a psychiatrist. I was appalled as I glanced over it.

According to the letter Eleanor had attempted to divorce her husband in the late 1940s. Due to this attempt she had been committed to a psychiatric hospital. The letter said things like, "Eleanor continues to fantasize about living on her own. Shock treatments have been unsuccessful; she continues to verbalize the desire to leave her husband." I later found a copy of a letter written by her husband to the psychiatrist refusing to pay the bill because they had not "fixed Eleanor." This attitude seemed so barbaric that I was truly stunned!

Eleanor was such a proud woman; I was sure she hadn't known those letters were in the boxes. Not wanting to embarrass her and feeling uncertain as to whether I should try to talk to her about what I had read, I carefully put them in the pile for her to look at, leaving it up to her to bring up the letters. She never did.

Through this sorting process I developed a newfound respect for Eleanor and all she had been through. I came to understand more fully her strong desire to remain independent and her insistence that she would not go into a nursing home, no matter what. I hoped for her sake that she would be able to stay in her home through her death. I knew it would devastate her to go back into an institution.

Eleanor never left her husband, but she did demonstrate how capable she was. She graduated with a Bachelor's Degree in Biology at a time when most women of her time did not go to college. After graduating she spent years doing research at a local college. When her husband died, she lived independently for many years providing for herself.

I was with Eleanor the day before she died. During this visit, I felt compelled to convey my admiration and respect for her. I made a point of telling her what a strong, capable woman she was and how she had inspired me to live a more courageous life. I saw gratitude on her face as I talked. Not knowing how to broach the topic of death, I asked, "Are you ready to go home, Eleanor?" This was my language, not hers. She gently took my hand and responded, "Cheryl, home is *wherever* you are."

I imagined the Eleanor of years before, locked up in the mental institution, and how she must have learned to "go within" when things were unbearable.

Is that what had sustained her through those months in the psychiatric hospital and was now helping her to stay so calm and peaceful as she was dying? I left that visit knowing I would never forget this incredible woman. Eleanor died that night in her home, just as she had hoped.

The day before her funeral I was walking around a mall, caught up in thoughts about Eleanor. I wondered if she had known she was going to die the night she died and whether she had been afraid. I hated the fact that she had died alone.

I have since learned that when someone is private, as Eleanor was, they often choose to die alone. But I didn't know that at the time, so I worried about her. Lost in thought, I found myself standing in front of a store window where I noticed a pewter butterfly key chain on display. I didn't need a keychain, but I felt drawn to it and bought it.

Later that night as I was taking my new purchase out of the bag, I noticed an inscription on the back of the butterfly. It was the Bible verse: 2 Cor. 5:17, and I felt the urge to look it up. Pulling out the little white Bible my Aunt had given me years before, I dusted it off and looked up the verse. It was about transformation. "Well," I thought, "How appropriate for a butterfly." With a happy heart and a smile on my face I tucked it away.

The next day was Eleanor's memorial. She had planned the entire service. Only a handful of people came, mostly hospice staff. It was sad to think that this vivacious, strong woman had only a few people left behind to remember her. She chose to have *Genesis* read as part of her service, as she loved the creation story. It was read by the hospice chaplain who went on to share that he had been with Eleanor a few days earlier in order to assist her in planning her funeral. During their meeting she picked songs and scripture to be read at her service. She faced her impending death just as she had lived her life— head on, with grace and dignity.

As he was leaving her that day the chaplain had stopped in her doorway and turned to her and asked, "Are you afraid to die, Eleanor?" She smiled at him and responded, "I think birth is a miracle." The chaplain, somewhat puzzled, replied, "Yes, birth is a miracle." With a peaceful look on her face she paused and then replied, "So is death." And that is how she left us, peaceful and certain that she was walking into another miracle.

According to the chaplain, Eleanor had only chosen one other verse to be read at her memorial. It was 2 Cor. 5: 17. When he said this I felt the hair stand up on the back of my neck and my body prickle with goose bumps. The verse read: "Old things are passed away; behold, all things become new," the same verse inscribed on the key chain I had bought. My initial thought was, "She wanted me to know she was okay." Then my logical mind stepped in and said, "Oh Cheryl, don't be silly. This is just a coincidence." It was the first of many, many such "coincidences" in my hospice career.

Home is Wherever You Are

As I reflect back on this experience and all the lessons I learned from Eleanor, the one thing that stands out the most for me is the importance of knowing "home is wherever you are." I have spent much time and energy in my life resisting *what is* and missing life by focusing on *how I want it to be instead* or wishing that it was *the way it used to be.*

When we fight against our current reality, we are actually giving our energy and attention to the things that we do not want. Psychologist Carl Jung famously said, "What you resist persists." This resistance actually draws more of what we don't want into our lives and fighting against "what is" drains our energy. When we relax into our current situation, we allow ourselves to be present to life.

The truth is that this moment is all that is certain. We don't know what will come tomorrow, and we cannot change what happened yesterday. So why not be at home right where we are? It really is all we have. It is only when we completely embrace the moment that we experience aliveness, relishing *what is* with no regrets about the past, and no worries about the future. It is from this place alone that we can fully live and feel the deliciousness of life. When we resist the fullness of the moment, we miss opportunities to connect with others, to be awed by the beauty of nature, to be guided, and to be at peace.

As I am writing this I stop to take a deep breath, and I look out the window. There, at my red nectar-filled feeder, is a vibrant green-throated hummingbird. I am filled with gratitude as I relax into this moment and know that I am home. Thank you, Eleanor.

Questions to Dance With...

What does the statement "home is wherever you are" mean to you?

When do you feel most at home?

Write about an area in your life that you may be resisting.

What can you do to feel more at home?

Seduction Of Safety

The greatest loss in life is not death.
The greatest loss is what dies inside us while we live.

~ Norman Cousins ~

THROUGHOUT MY HOSPICE CAREER, I'VE worked with many Jewish families. I was mesmerized as I sat with them and listened to the stories of their ancestors. These were tales of sacrifice and strong faith. Many of them had relatives who had died in the Holocaust and some had experienced these horrors firsthand. I was inspired by their stories as well as the love and devotion they had for one another.

I was also moved by the fact that, in spite of the persecution their family members had endured, their faith continued to be strong. They had grown up immersed in the Jewish faith, and they firmly believed what they had been taught. As I came to know these families, I found myself questioning what I was being taught in the Christian faith.

The Jewish families I worked with believed what they had been raised to believe, just as my Christian friends had. They were just as passionate about their beliefs, just as committed to their families, and just as loving and kind. Yet I was being taught that Jewish people would be condemned because of their beliefs. As a result, I began to question and more deeply examine the spiritual teaching that I was being exposed to.

Many of the Jewish families I worked with were incredibly loving, but there were also families who were struggling in life because of their own trauma around the war and its aftermath. Klaus's family was one of the latter. He was diagnosed with a lung disease called COPD. His wife, Madeline, was his caregiver. She was a feisty German woman who had married a man whom, she confessed to me, she should have never married. He was twenty years her senior. Madeline told me that she had been drawn to him because he provided safety and security. She chose not to have children, not wanting to bring them into a loveless marriage.

Madeline's parents had been killed in a concentration camp when she was a young girl. Although guarded when talking about her childhood, she did acknowledge that she was drawn to the fatherly way Klaus treated her because of the trauma she had experienced as a child. She said that she didn't love him the way she thought a wife should love her husband, but she always drew solace from knowing that she would have financial security and freedom after he was gone. Klaus lived well into his 90s and Madeline felt trapped in her marriage. With her limited education, lack of marketable skills, and her self-confessed insecurity, she felt ill-equipped to live without him.

She talked to me about how needy and demanding her husband was and how she felt she had lost herself in their relationship. She expressed regrets about lost dreams. She had wanted to be an artist at one point in her life but let it go because her husband saw art as silly and frivolous. She said to me, "He expected the house to be spotless and dinner to be on the table when he got home. He did not want his wife 'wasting her time'." For years their relationship had been more like a parent-child relationship, with Klaus being a stern father figure. She fantasized about leaving him many times but did not know how she could take care of herself. This fear kept her in the marriage.

As he grew sicker, she felt the strain of providing care for a man she held a great deal of resentment towards. She was worn out by his constant demands but felt she had an obligation to him after forty years of marriage. They lived in a luxurious, pristine home, which had come to feel like a prison to Madeline. She was anxious and stressed. Knowing they had the funds to hire a caregiver, I encouraged her to get additional help. Klaus did not want anyone but Madeline to provide care to him. She was resigned to caring for him, as she felt it was her "duty" as his wife.

Klaus was rigid and demanding. He expected things to be done in a very specific way and would let people know if they misstepped. They had hired housekeepers in the past, but Klaus always fired them, as they never did things as thoroughly as he felt they should. Madeline was under the same scrutiny and reported always feeling criticized, never feeling like she could do anything well enough to satisfy her husband. I guess that I should not have been surprised by Klaus' response to my overtures to get him to talk about his life. He was extremely guarded in sharing his history. He would only say that the past should remain in the past.

Both Klaus and Madeline spent time privately with me, processing their frustration with each other. Klaus complained that his wife was not being an adequate caregiver. She shared that he was verbally abusive at times, telling her how lazy or stupid he thought she was. Whenever I was with the two of them together, they were always civil towards each other. They had learned from years of practice how to put up a good front. Although Madeline had never left Klaus, I wondered if he was aware at some level of her disdain for him.

It saddened me to witness these two people in their "golden years" spending their days feeling unhappy and resentful. I spent time with each of them, listening to the many regrets they both seemed to have. I encouraged them to sit down with me together so they could talk through some of their feelings. Although they both resisted, I continued to work toward opening up this communication.

Unfortunately, they never got the chance to do that. Madeline died very suddenly of a heart attack. Since Klaus was our hospice patient and much older than Madeline, this was a shock to all of us. Knowing all that I did about her and how she felt about her life and her marriage, I felt heartsick that she had died so unfulfilled.

I was surprised by the strength of Klaus's reaction to her death. He was absolutely devastated. I have since learned from this experience and subsequent ones that unresolved issues between people can often complicate the survivor's grief experience. Although they did not have a healthy relationship, I do believe he loved her. As he processed his wife's death, he appeared to be clueless about how unhappy she had been in their marriage. If he had known about her feelings, he was not willing to discuss them.

After her death, he became fearful about who was going to take care of him. He had the means to hire caregivers to meet his basic needs, but they could not replace the care that his wife had been giving. (After all, he had trained her well.) Due to his demanding and angry way of being, he went through many different caregivers in the last months of his life.

Although he was hard on his caregivers, he was usually kind to me. He continued to ask me to visit. I believe he felt a connection to me because I had spent time with Madeline before she passed. In the last couple of weeks of his life, I watched him soften. His wife's death seemed to put things in perspective for him. When he died, I wondered if Madeline had the ability to greet him on the other side— and if she did, whether she would be willing to.

Safety is Overrated

This was a tough case for me. Madeline was miserable but could not see past her current circumstances. She was immersed in victimhood. She was not willing to look at where she could take responsibility in her own life and had grown accustomed to making her husband the villain who ruined her life while she played the role of martyr. Both Klaus and Madeline were unhappy, yet neither was willing to take responsibility for the part they played in their loveless relationship.

I understood that Madeline may not have been able to see a way out and had fear about what her life might be like if she left him. In staying with Klaus she at least "knew what she was getting." After years of working with child abuse, I've learned that children living in abusive homes often want to stay right there because that abuse is all they have ever known. Their fear of the unknown is stronger than their desire to get out of the violent situation. So, I did understand where she was coming from. But it was also true that she had made a choice. She had chosen Klaus to be her dance partner in life.

She had chosen to dance that dance that came with the presumed security of knowing all the steps beforehand, instead of choosing a dance option that allowed her to learn a new dance . . . or a series of new dances over the years. Her fear of the unknown future, based on her personal background, overrode her personal desire to get more out of life.

After witnessing the terms of this marriage, it was clear to me that "safety" can be highly overrated. Madeline spent forty years of her life feeling trapped, angry, and resentful. I believe that's what killed her. If she had left Klaus, she might not have lived the privileged life she had grown accustomed to or driven luxury vehicles, but she would have been free.

This experience made me take a good hard look at where, in my own life, I was playing it safe. I had been feeling dissatisfied with life for quite a while, feeling that something was missing for me. I was born and raised in Nebraska and knew nothing else. I had been living a safe, comfortable life. After seeing the results of playing it safe, I was motivated to take a risk. Within a year of completing my internship, I left a ten-year position with the state of Nebraska, sold the house I had been living in for eight years, and moved to California without knowing a soul or having a job lined up. Moving opened my life up in ways that I could have never imagined, and I have never regretted my decision.

I could have easily stayed, but I would have always wondered. We often feel trapped by our circumstances. For me, leaving a job where I had invested ten years of my life and had wonderful benefits seemed ill-advised, even ludicrous. Knowing I would have to start over from scratch in another position might have stopped me. Selling my 1800 sq. ft. home on a quarter-acre of land and knowing I wouldn't be able to afford to buy in California might have stopped me. These were hard decisions. But I knew that the choices I was making were even more far-reaching than they appeared to be.

I understand that our life choices can be extremely difficult. I have often wondered if Madeline had had the chance to live her life over again, if she would have made different choices. Unfortunately, she can't. But as long as we are still on this planet, in these bodies, we have choice. Even if our parents die in a concentration camp, or we get locked in a psychiatric ward, we have choice in how we "show up." Victim, martyr, or hero? We get to choose. So, I ask you, where are you playing it safe?

Questions to Dance With...

Are there areas in your life where you feel unhappy or feel you are settling?
Pick one and write about it.

What choices do you have regarding this situation? Write them down
even if they are not ideal.

If you made these choices how might your life change? I invite you to use
your imagination here.

Mothers and Daughters

*Sometimes the strength of motherhood
is greater than natural laws.*

~ Barbara Kingsolver ~

WHEN I MOVED TO CALIFORNIA it was a huge leap of faith. I didn't know a soul and had no job or place to live. Although a majority of my social work experience was with child protective services, I felt called to work for hospice and chose to apply only for hospice positions. Within a few weeks of moving, I was offered a position as a hospice bereavement counselor. I had rented a cute little two-bedroom apartment before I knew where I was going to work and ended up living just a few miles from my new office. Everything came together so easily that it felt like a sign that I was on the right track. Soon after starting my new position I began to have experiences and hear stories from families that made me ask the questions that had come up repeatedly as an intern. I asked, "Is there life after death? If there is, can those who have passed on communicate with the living?" When I worked with Eleanor during my internship, I had felt that she had sent me a message after her death. I discovered in my work with bereaved families that I was not the only one who felt they received messages from beyond the grave.

One cool autumn morning, I continued my journey into the world of unexplained happenings. I had two bereavement assessments scheduled in a row. My first appointment was with a woman named Kelly, whose mother had died while on our hospice program. After spending some time sharing her feelings of sadness, Kelly began to tell me about the night her mother died. She shared this:

> *"The night Mom died I stayed with her in her room. I knew she was getting close to the end of her life. I didn't want her to die alone. She had not been responding for a few days. She looked like a little bird, so tiny in that big hospital bed surrounded by pillows. I hated to see her in this condition. She had always been such a strong woman. I sat with her for hours, and each breath seemed like it might be her last. Sometime in the early morning hours, I drifted off to sleep in the chair next to her. I dreamt that I woke up and looked over at my mother and was surprised to see the covers pulled over her head. There was no movement; my heart stopped. She had been much too weak to even move. I carefully pulled the covers down. My mother was lying there with her eyes wide open. She slowly turned her head to look at me, then reached out and gently touched my face. She said softly, "Thank you for taking care of me."*

> *It was at that instant, I jerked awake with a start. I looked over at my mother, who was motionless. I sensed that something had changed and rushed to her side. She was not breathing but her body was still warm. I could still feel her hand on my cheek. I knew that she had just told me goodbye. My mother was not an affectionate person. She did not show appreciation or gratitude. The fact that she had thanked me was huge. I will never forget that tender moment with her."*

I was moved by Kelly's story. As she shared her dream, I had goose bumps. She shared a sacred and precious moment that she had had with her mother. Was it real? Had her mother come to her in a dream? I didn't think so. I believed it was her grief or her strong desire to have closure. I didn't think her mom had actually come to her, but I knew that Kelly believed that she had.

Later that afternoon, I had another visit scheduled, again with a woman who had recently lost her mother. Amy was distraught. She shed many tears and had lots of questions. She was struggling with the fact that a hospice nurse had advised her to tell her mother it was okay to go. She said she was not comfortable doing this but didn't want her mother to hold on if she wanted to go. So one day she went into her mother's room and sat on the side of her bed and said, "Mom, you know it's okay to go." She said her mother's eyes shot open and she turned to her daughter angrily and said "NO!" Amy was tortured by this. She hoped that her mother knew that she wanted her to live. She just didn't want her to suffer.

I've heard many well-meaning hospice staff encourage people to tell their loved ones that it's okay to go. I prefer to let people know that, although for some people this is helpful, it is best for them to use their own judgment as to whether this is something that their loved one needs to hear. They know their family member and the relationship they have with them better than anyone.

It is the job of hospice staff to educate people so they can make informed decisions. It is not our job to tell people what they need to do. Family members have a lifetime of experiences with the dying person. Usually, hospice staff have only known the patient for a few months, weeks or even days. We are not the best judges of what should be said. Each family is unique and must be treated so.

The most amazing part of my visit with Amy was the story she told me at the end of our visit. This is what she shared:

> *"Mom had been out of it for a few days. I had been staying with her day and night. After several days without sleep I called my brother Rusty and asked him to come and sit with Mom so I could go home to get a few hours' sleep. I was exhausted and went to sleep as soon as my head hit the pillow. And then, I had the most incredible dream. I dreamt that my mom was standing in front of me. She was wearing a gorgeous*

white flowing gown. She just stood there looking at me. She looked radiant, healthier and happier than I had seen her in years. She gave me this huge smile and then she turned and began walking up this beautiful spiral staircase that seem to come from nowhere. I began to follow her up the stairs but she stopped, turned around and held out her hand to stop me. Whispering, "No sweetheart, I have to go alone from here." At that moment, the phone woke me up. It was Rusty. He called to say "Mom just took her last breath."

In a matter of a couple of hours I had been with two women who both believed with every fiber of their beings that their mothers had come to them at the moment of their death to say goodbye.

After meeting with Kelly, I had wondered whether her mother had really visited her, or if this perceived event came from her grief and the need to have closure. I left my second assessment of the day with Amy questioning my own doubting mind.

Since meeting Kelly and Amy, I have heard hundreds of stories about people being visited by their deceased loved ones in their dreams. They often say, "It wasn't like any dream I've had before." These dreams tend to be extraordinarily vivid and clear. People describe them in great detail. Some include tactile experiences, like Kelly's dream in which she felt her mom's hand on her cheek. Often these dreams coincide with the actual time of death of the loved one. Remarkably, these are dreams that are often remembered in detail even years later.

Pay Attention to Your Dreams

It was because of the many experiences that I've had that I began to pay closer attention to things that, for most of my life, I had paid no mind to. For years I had ignored my dreams as just meaningless rants of my mind while I was in an unconscious state. I have begun to wonder over the years if the opposite isn't true . . . that in this "unconscious" state the other realms of being are perhaps more accessible to us.

In order to become more aware of my dreams, I began to make a conscious effort to start my days at a slower pace. Rather than charge into my days as I had done for so long, I began to ease into my mornings. Initially I journaled about my dream of the night before, but as I continued to observe this quiet time in the mornings I started to tap into other dreams that brought me face to face with the longing of my soul. At that point the message to "pay attention to my dreams" took on a deeper meaning.

I knew that being aware of what happened during my sleep was only one piece of the puzzle. I became aware that, by slowing down and paying attention to what was going on within me, I was able to access my soul's longing. This book was germinated in those early morning journaling sessions. (Okay, in all honesty, the sessions didn't happen all that early— I'm really not a morning person!) But when I did get up, I took time to be in silence, to connect with my soul, and to remember my dreams. As I did this, I began to feel more grounded and to have more clarity about my life.

I encourage you to take time each day to "be" with yourself. Explore your dreams, your desires and your feelings through journaling. This can be a healing and soothing time, a time of rejuvenation and preparation for the day ahead—or a way to cleanse yourself at the end of the day from the inside out. Answering the following questions may help you to begin your own exploration.

Questions to Dance With...

Describe in detail a vivid dream you have had. It could be about a loved one— or anyone or anything else that comes to mind. If you don't remember your dreams, write about a dream you have for your life.

What does this dream mean to you?

Describe a time when you felt that you received a message through your dreams.

Back to Life

We are all so much together, but we are all dying of loneliness.

~ Albert Schweitzer ~

WHEN I MET FLORENCE, I was sure she wasn't going to live more than a few weeks. She was a ninety-four-year-old woman who weighed less than 90 pounds. She lived in a little run-down trailer by herself. Her home was dark and dingy, and most days she barely got out of bed.

We were told by her niece Deanne, her only living relative, to let ourselves in as Florence would not come to the door and kept a key hidden under the mat. Deanne was a single parent and lived in a two-bedroom apartment with her three small children. Because of her limited space she was unable to bring Florence to her home. Once a week she prepared meals and left them for Florence to warm up but was not able to offer much more than that. Florence rarely ate the food she brought her. Deanne was desperate to get help for her aunt.

Florence was not safe to be alone in her weakened state but had no money for caregivers or a nursing home. There were programs she could apply for to get assistance but she had not done so. In order to ensure her safety until arrangements, could be made for her to go into a nursing home, the hospice team began to take turns going to her home. We sent out a nurse and nurses' aides on a daily basis and arranged for a couple of volunteers to go in several days a week to cook meals and keep her company. Deanne agreed to increase her visits, as well. The chaplain and I were also going to her home a couple of days a week. This plan was a temporary fix to give Deanne time to complete the paperwork to get Florence admitted into a nursing home.

Florence had had little human interaction over the last couple of years. Deanne admitted that even when she visited, it was usually a quick stop to drop off food as she had to tend to her children. Her hospice diagnosis was "failure to thrive" with a secondary diagnosis of congestive heart failure. Failure to thrive is a diagnosis often given to babies when they are neglected and without sufficient interaction. They stop eating and appear to lose the will to live. In Florence's case, I sensed that she was dying of loneliness and had simply given up on life.

When I first met her she primarily stayed in bed and had little to say. She was weak and withdrawn. If I tried to engage her in conversation she would pull the sheets over her head, making it clear that she wanted to be left alone. She had a faraway look in her eyes and was difficult to engage. The nurse who examined her assessed that she would not live more than a few weeks due of her fragile state.

On my first couple of visits with Florence, I would find her back in her tiny bedroom with the covers pulled over her head and the shades drawn. I had the impression that I was bothering her every time I attempted to talk to her, and the other team members were reporting the same thing. Then something incredible happened. Within a week of hospice getting involved she began to get up and "dress for her company." She started putting on makeup and fixing her hair. She began engaging in conversation about her life, telling colorful stories of her days as an actress in the 1930s and her many romances. As she reviewed her life I felt honored to be with her. Those glazed-over eyes began to shine brightly. She had come back to life before our eyes.

After a few weeks, she was doing so well that she no longer met the criteria for failure to thrive and no longer needed to go into a nursing home. She had reconnected with life and was not only eating again, she seemed to savor every bite. She continued on our hospice service with a diagnosis of congestive heart failure. Over the next several months she demonstrated a zest for life that surprised us, as it was such a stark contrast from the woman we first met.

I am happy to tell you that Florence spent her last few months reveling in the attention she received from all her visitors. It was beautiful to witness as she re-engaged and began to dance with life once again.

It is not uncommon for people who are isolated to withdraw and even will themselves to die. All Florence needed was to be connected, to be touched, to know that people cared about her, and her life began to have purpose and color again.

I am so glad that Florence decided to come out from under the covers to give us all a chance to know her. We were captivated by her as she moved elegantly through her final days. What an honor it was to be a part of the team that helped her connect with her love of life again and to be one of her supportive partners as she gracefully completed her final dance.

We Need Each Other

The lesson was clear with Florence: we need each other. For many of us the relationships we have with others gives the greatest meaning to our lives. Lacking human connection, Florence felt she had no purpose. No amount of treatment or medication could restore that purpose. After we entered her life, she made a choice. She got up, got dressed, put her make-up on and stepped back into life. When I reflect back on Florence's situation, it a clear example of how human interaction can impact our functioning. I believe that due to Florence's isolation she concluded that she didn't matter. She found herself with nothing to live for or focus on.

Her niece had described her as "fiercely independent." I myself have often proudly proclaimed that I am an independent woman, and I know that there are many who can relate to this. We live in a society that teaches us not to show our true feelings, a society that values toughness and personal independence.

There is a serious downside to the kind of independence that we are taught to cultivate. For one thing, the independent, "I don't need anyone" approach to life is often a lonely one (I can attest to this personally.) For another, independence can easily breed disconnection, and emotional disconnection can have a cumulative effect over time.

It hasn't always been this way. We used to take care of our own, but in the seventies, there was a big shift as books such as *Co-dependent No More* became popular. Of course, I do believe it's true that we can become "too dependent" on another, especially when we look at another as the key to our happiness. But it seems that through this movement the pendulum had swung too far to the left. We began to see healthy connections and needing each other as a bad thing, proudly proclaiming that we don't need anyone!

I see the sad results of such "independence" or emotional disconnection all too often in my hospice work. I caution us all on two counts. First, let us not be too quick to push away offers of help and support that we receive along the away. Second, it is a good thing to let people know when we need them and to reach out when we're struggling. Disconnection from others happens when we're too intent on cultivating our independence and keeping a stiff upper lip.

The result can be that when we need people the most, we may have become so disconnected that we end up alone and isolated. The more isolated we become, the harder it is to reach out. When we do this, our world can get really small. I believe that was the case with Florence.

As a woman who has never married and always prided herself in not needing others, I know this independence well. I also find myself isolating when I am writing in order to have the space to create. But as I spent time with Florence I was reminded of how important my outside connections are. They feed my creativity and satisfy my need to belong. We all want to know that we matter. Even the most introverted person needs human contact in order to feel fully alive.

As I have seen the results of the "I don't need anyone" attitude in my hospice patients over the years, I've realized the importance of building a support network. I've learned to lean on others and ask for help, allowing myself to be more honest and vulnerable in my relationships. This authenticity has deepened and strengthened my relationships. As I allow others into my life, the good times feel even happier and the challenges manageable. I reach out to the hand that reaches out to me, and we balance and support each other. Opening to others has enhanced and brightened my life, just as Florence's dark, dingy trailer became a place where love emerged.

Questions to Dance With...

How do you feel about depending on others or asking for help?

Is there an area in your life where you could use support? Describe it.

Who are the people in your life you can reach out to when you need support?

Dressed for God

Attitude is a little thing that makes a big difference.

~Winston Churchill~

MY PATIENTS HAVE BEEN AND continue to be my greatest teachers. One inspiring example of how to live and treat others came from my patient Greg. He demonstrated how a person's attitude can have a positive impact on the quality of life for those around him, as well as his own.

Greg had a strong faith in God. He told me once that he had always wanted to be a minister. When he was widowed a few years earlier, his sister Sue, who had never married, moved in with him. She cooked and cleaned for him and, in exchange, he provided her room and board.

Over the first few weeks that I worked with Greg, he declined rapidly. It became evident that he was getting too weak to be at home without additional care. Although Sue was willing to care for him, she was too frail once he was in a wheelchair. He had told me he had limited resources, so hiring caregivers was not an option. I knew it was time to talk to him about going into a nursing home, so I gently broached the topic.

Oftentimes this conversation is met with resistance, and sometimes even anger, but that wasn't so with Greg. He readily agreed that it was time for him to go into a nursing home. It took me aback when he actually seemed excited about the prospect and said, "I have always wanted to do missionary work, so maybe this is my opportunity." His only real concern was for his sister.

Greg had been living in a lovely condo with charming bay windows and a captivating view of his garden. If he had sold his home, he could have afforded to live in a much nicer nursing facility. He didn't want to sell it because he wanted Sue to have a place to live after his death.

I learned a lot from Greg as I watched him in his last few months of life. Many of my patients who go into nursing homes fall into a depression or simply give up once they get there. But Greg was different. Although the halls of this facility reeked of Pine-sol (the go-to disinfectant this nursing home used in an attempt to cover the not-so-subtle odors that are common in nursing homes), Greg rarely complained. For him, being there was an opportunity to be of service to others. Although he saw this as an opportunity to do his "missionary work," he did not proselytize or preach to the residents. He simply loved them. He learned their names and made a point of greeting each resident as he passed them in the hallways. If someone was having a bad day, Greg would be by their side to offer comfort. He was a living expression of love, and people were drawn to him.

As he got closer to the end of his life his main concern continued to be for his sister Sue. He wanted to make sure she would be taken care of. In Greg's last week he grew weaker and became bedbound. His sister was at his side every day. He stopped eating as his body was no longer able to process food, so he deteriorated rapidly. Within a week of becoming bedridden he died.

The day after his death I called to check on Sue. I expected to hear the pain and sorrow that I often hear when I make these calls. To my surprise, she sounded elated. She shared with me that she had gone to see Greg the day he died and was shocked to see that he had more energy than he had had in several days. When she walked into his room she said he was so excited he could hardly contain himself. He told her that he'd had the most glorious morning, explaining that he had walked in the garden and had a delicious steak for lunch. She was totally surprised to hear this because Greg had not been able to eat anything for days and had been too weak to walk.

He went on to tell her that he had an incredible experience in the garden. He said, "God talked to me today and told me that I don't have to worry about you as he will be looking out for you." She said that his eyes were shining brightly with excitement as he talked to her. He had been anxious during the previous few days, but Sue said that she saw no anxiety in him that morning. He was peaceful and happy.

As Sue was getting ready to leave that day, he asked her to first help him change into his favorite white cotton shirt. His joy was infectious as she helped him get into his Sunday best. He smiled and waved as she left. She felt uplifted by the visit. As she was leaving she checked with the nurses to confirm what Greg had told her – they informed her that Greg had not eaten nor been out of his room. She was shocked when less than thirty minutes after walking out of the nursing home, she received the call telling her that Greg had died. But the next moment found her grinning because she realized that her brother had wanted to put on his best shirt to meet God. Although the brother whom she dearly loved had died, Sue maintained her equanimity.

I was deeply touched by her attitude which I would describe as joyful and optimistic, even enthusiastic. She was simply delighted for Greg . . sure that he had spent the morning jubilantly dancing with God, who then took him home.

Our Attitude Impacts Our Experience

As I continued my work with the dying, I began a journey of self-exploration. I became more and more introspective. I found myself wondering why people have such drastically different experiences in life and death. Why do some people suffer so much while others seem to have blessed lives in which everything flows easily for them?

I often observed that there seemed to be a continuity between how people experienced life prior to their illness and how they moved through their dying process. When I saw patients who eased gracefully into their deaths, I would ask myself, "Did things flow so beautifully at the end of their lives because they had a good attitude? Or did they have a great attitude because things flowed so easily for them? Which came first?

Greg demonstrated how powerful an impact his way of thinking or attitude had on his life. Ending up in a nursing home is not what anyone wants at the end of their life. But Greg saw his move into the nursing facility as an opportunity. Because he viewed this move in a positive way, he continued to be lighthearted. I believe he truly enjoyed his time in the nursing home as he took his final opportunity to do missionary work, making the most of the last few months of his life.

What I have seen over the years is that patient's thoughts and attitudes directly influence how they experience their last days. Greg was a great example of this. The reality is that all of my hospice patients have been diagnosed with a terminal illness— not exactly a prime example of "things going well." Yet some of my patients have handled themselves and their journey to the end with real grace and dignity. Others have gone out kicking and screaming.

Those who struggle seem to spend more time worrying about what could go wrong. They are anxious about what is to come, or they obsess over what isn't— all they didn't get to do or will miss doing. Those who take the approach of dealing with what comes one day at a time seem to have a smoother and easier passage than those who fret and worry.

I've also come to realize that it's the quality of the questions people are asking that influence the level of distress they experience. As I help them process what's happening to them, those who are struggling often ask, "Why is this happening to me? What have I done to deserve this?" They see themselves as victims- a stance that I recognize easily, as I have lived from the place of victimhood for a large portion of my life. The *victim* feels embattled, so they fight against the reality of *what is.*

On the other hand, patients who handle their terminal status with less struggle ask themselves questions such as, "What gifts are in this experience for me? What are my priorities- what do I really want to do with the time I have left?"

I knew that I needed to pay attention to this, and that I could use this awareness to live my life with less struggle and more joy. It was one of those *aha* moments for me. It became apparent to me that my thoughts and attitudes were impacting my life, making the changes didn't come so easily. I had to make a conscious effort to notice my thoughts and have the courage to see when I was taking a "lower road" in my thinking.

One example of this happened about nine years ago. I had decided to take a year-long trip around the world with my boyfriend Derek. I was already working on changing my thoughts and what I focused on in life (gratitude vs. problems). I felt that the trip around the world was a direct manifestation of this shift in thinking. It was also a direct result of working with the dying and learning lessons like the *Do it NOW!* lesson I had learned. But as life would have it, three and a half months into this amazing trip, Derek broke up with me. This had not been part of what I had hoped to create. I ended my trip early and decided to move to Hawaii (since I had quit my job and sold everything I owned in order to take this trip).

It wasn't until I arrived on the island of Oahu that reality of what had happened set in. In the midst of this drama, I found myself slipping back into old ways of being and thinking. I called my friend Mica and began to sob, saying things like, "I gave up everything for him! I can't believe he did this to me!" I went on and on about how he behaved on the trip. I found myself immersed in victimhood. She allowed me to go on for a while and then she stopped me in my tracks when she asked, "Who is this?" Shocked, I paused, and she asked again, "Who is this and what did you do with my friend Cheryl?" Her question stopped my ranting. She then asked, "Cheryl, is this who you were being on the trip? Because if it is, this is not the woman Derek left with."

Initially, I felt very annoyed her response, wanting her to commiserate with me. But when I took pause and honestly looked at the situation, I realized that she was right. While we were traveling I had gotten into a lot of fear. I had never traveled in third world countries where I, as a woman, was treated like a second-class citizen. There was also stress around money as I was using my life savings for the trip. Derek and I had both lived alone prior to the trip, and suddenly found ourselves together 24/7. As much as I hated to admit it, I had become an anxious and negative travel partner. I responded to Mica, "Yes, this is who I was being." It was in that moment that I stepped back into my power. Once I stopped blaming and took responsibility for my part in how things turned out, I was able to shift my thinking from "Poor me" to "Now what?" From that place, the place that Greg had modeled beautifully for me, I was able recreate my life in a powerful way.

To take this point even deeper, I want to share a story I heard about a man who was the gatekeeper of a village. The village was surrounded by a big wall and his job was to open the gate as people entered and left the city. One afternoon an older gentleman came to the village. As he was entering, he asked the gate keeper, "What are the people like who live in this village?" The gatekeeper asked, "What were the people like in the village you used to live in?" He responded, "They were selfish and self-centered. It was each man for himself!" The gatekeeper responded, "That is how you will find the people in this village as well."

Later that same day another man came to the village. He, too, asked the gatekeeper, "What are the people like in this village?" The gatekeeper again asked, "What are they like in the village you are coming from?" The man responded, "Oh they are wonderful! Everyone is so caring and generous. People really look out for each other." The gatekeeper replied, "That is how you will find them here as well."

The story's lesson is clear: You will find whatever you are looking for. And so it is in life. If you expect the worst, that is what you will experience. I see it with hospice patients: if they expect to struggle and suffer, they probably will. If they believe that their last days offer the opportunity to grow closer to their family members, they probably will. If they express gratitude for their blessings and trust that things will flow easily for them, then that is what they will experience. Of course, this doesn't mean that they won't experience periods of discomfort, but their attitudes can impact how they respond to those moments and shift their experience.

It's the same for all of us. We can't control everything that happens to us, but we can control how we respond to it. We can become aware of our thoughts and attitude and the significant role they play in creating our feelings. When we are aware of our negative thoughts and shift what we are thinking, we can positively impact our attitude and how we show up in the world.

Questions to Dance With...

Identify an area in your life that is difficult or isn't working as well as you would like it to and elaborate on it. (finances, romance, creativity, etc.)

Write about some of the things you think or say about this situation. Can you see any correlation between your attitude toward this situation and the outcome?

What gifts are in this experience? If my patients can find gifts in their dying process, I have complete faith that you can find the gifts that are imbedded in your challenges!

Winged Messages

If you aren't living in awe then you aren't paying attention.
~ Dan Millman ~

The Crow

A S I CONTINUED MY WORK with dying patients and their grieving family members, I heard more and more stories about unusual experiences people were having around the death of their loved ones. I soon discovered that dreams were not the only way that people believed their loved ones communicated with them after their deaths. I heard stories about rainbows, cloud formations, dragonflies, and birds carrying special messages. I myself had several experiences involving birds and butterflies. But I had never had a shared experience until one Saturday afternoon when we experienced that kind of magic in the bereavement group I was facilitating.

We were sitting in a conference room with our chairs in a circle underneath the skylight in order to enjoy the afternoon sun. There was a young man in the group named Paul who had lost his sister, Julie. She had died in a car accident. He talked about how vibrant and full of life she had been and how difficult it was to believe she was gone. He shared that she had a fascination for crows.

Because of her fondness for these birds, Julie's family even put crows on her funeral program, which Paul brought in to show the group. As he passed around the program, he told us that while they were standing around the casket at the graveside these huge crows circled all around them during the service. Paul said that everyone at the service had commented on how strangely they were behaving. He said he believed that she had come back through the crows or had somehow sent the crows to let him and the rest of her family know she was okay.

We were moved by his story, but what really brought the story to life for us was when a huge crow appeared on the skylight above us. This enormous crow kept hopping up and down, cawing loudly as only crows can do. I had been doing groups in that room for a couple of years and had never once heard nor seen a bird up there on the skylight. This crow was obnoxious. It made its presence known for the entire time that Paul was telling his story. Then as soon as he finished sharing the crow flew away. No one in the room said a word about the crow until I did. Then everyone started laughing, seemingly relieved that I had stated the obvious. One of the group participants said, "Oh my God, it was freaking me out!" As all heads nodded, it was clear that everyone had been aware that the crow had been there, but apparently no one had wanted to "sound crazy" by being the one to point it out.

That was a goose bump moment for me. I had heard so many stories of birds over the ears and had even had some personal encounters with birds in relationship to death. This was the first time I had had such a shared experience. It was a powerful day. Although some people might feel this was just a coincidence, I don't. For many years that would have been my response, as well. But now, after years of "coincidences" such as that one, I have no doubt that they are so much more.

Swooping Hawks

Throughout my career in hospice I have experienced or heard about many "signs from the grave" that are manifested by nature. Sometimes after I've had an unusual encounter with a bird, I will find out that one of my patients has died in the night or over the weekend.

One such experience happened on a lazy Sunday afternoon as I was lying in bed reading with the curtains open so that I could enjoy the canyon view. That particular day I was startled when two huge hawks swooped down past my first-floor window. They flew so close to the window that if I had stuck my hand out, they would have hit it. I sat at the edge of my bed watching as these two hawks played together in the breeze.

Once again, they came swooping by my window and I felt goose bumps run up my arms. I had a clear sense that something special was happening as I watched them, like two synchronized swimmers, make a third pass by my window, and I had the thought, "Ed must have died."

I had worked in hospice for several years when this happened and already had many experiences linking birds and death, so I wasn't surprised when I went into work on Monday morning to learn that Ed had, in fact, died on Sunday morning. What took me by surprise was the news that his wife Beth (who wasn't a hospice patient) had died four hours after his death.

I had been working with Beth to support her in preparing emotionally for her husband's death. As I learned this news my mind immediately flashed back to the beautiful scene of the two hawks swooping by my bedroom window. I knew that I had had another visit.

Songs of Love

One afternoon I was talking with my friend Dawn, whom I had known for twenty years, about some of the interesting experiences I have had around birds. She was silent for a time and then she said, "I have never shared this with anyone before, but . . ." She then went on to share about the morning after her brother Bobbie had died tragically in a fire. In all the years I had known her, she had never told me this story.

The day after Bobbie's death she and her parents went to his home, trying to make sense of what had happened. Dawn said that as they were walking around the house looking at the damage, they became aware of a little robin that seemed to be following them around. She said, "It appeared to be unafraid, staying close to us the entire time we were at the house. It would come right up to us." The bird's behavior was so unusual that she and her parents all commented on it.

That night she stayed with her parents and the next morning when she woke up she was surprised to see a little robin fluttering in front of the bedroom window. The bird began to sing, and she said she heard the words "I love you, I love you, I love you" within the bird's song. She thought she must be imagining things, so was very surprised when she went downstairs and her mom began sharing about her experience that morning.

Dawn's mom said that she was in the kitchen making breakfast when she noticed a robin sitting on the window sill. She went on to tell Dawn that when the bird began to sing she heard the words, "I love you Mom, I love you Mom, I love you Mom" within the bird's song. Dawn said that for several days after this the robin stayed close by and whenever they sat outside it would come right up to them. They both felt sure that it was a sign from Bobbie.

After Dawn told me about her experience she said this: "I never tell anyone about the robin. I don't want people to think we're nuts." Hearing my stories about signs from birds had been reassuring to her. Not only had these stories given her permission to share her own experience, but it also validated the experience she and her mom had.

Butterfly Kisses

While on a trip to Bali I had the privilege of witnessing a dear friend's magical encounter with a butterfly. We were lying out by a swimming pool, bathing in the tropical sun, when this brilliant azure blue and black butterfly came floating by.

As we lay next to each other, the butterfly flitted around my friend Thomas. It circled around him for several minutes and then landed on his foot. We thought it was cool but didn't give it any significance. After about ten minutes it left his foot, circled around him again, and then landed on his arm.

The butterfly never came near me but it sure seemed to be drawn to

Thomas. After sitting on his arm for quite a while, the butterfly appeared to start flying away, only to turn around and circle around Thomas for the third time. It then landed on his forehead, where it stayed for about twenty minutes or so. We were amazed by this butterfly's behavior. I had the sense that this was more than just a chance encounter with a friendly butterfly.

Thomas sensed it too and whispered, "I think it's my mom." I looked over at him to see tears streaming down his face. He had lost both his parents and his only sibling within a five-year period. Even though he had been closer to his father than his mother, his intuition told him that this was a sign from his mother. It was clear to me, as well, that this was a holy moment, so much so that tears began streaming down my face. I knew how much this encounter meant to Thomas and truly felt honored to be a witness to this beautiful interaction.

A few years after this experience I was watching a video of Wayne Dyer talking about his book, *Inspiration: Your Ultimate Calling*. In it he shared about his friend Jack Boland, who had a fascination with monarch butterflies. After his friend died, Dyer decided to include a story Jack had told him about a monarch butterfly in his next book. On the morning that he finished writing the story, he had an encounter with a monarch butterfly while walking on the beach. This tenacious butterfly landed on his finger and ended up staying with him for several hours. Dyer firmly believed that the monarch butterfly was a direct message or a messenger from his friend Jack. I was flooded with gratitude after I'd heard Dyer's story because it was another validation of the experiences I'd been having.

Now I don't want you to get the impression that every time I see a bird or a butterfly I think that someone has died! There is much more to the experience than just seeing these winged creatures. The hair stands up on the back of my neck or I get goose bumps, similar to what happens when I am near a patient as they take their last breath. Often the birds or the butterflies do not behave in a typical manner and I am aware on a spiritual level that something else is going on. Interestingly, I don't have these experiences every time a patient dies. They are much more likely to happen when I've established a deeper relationship.

Allow Yourself to Be Vulnerable

Over the years, I have learned how essential it is to share our experiences. And that's one of the main reasons I have written this book. When we tell our stories, we pave the way for others to share theirs. This is the lesson I've been privileged to revisit over and over again as I've facilitated grief support groups.

The more vulnerable my bereavement clients are in the group the deeper the group goes. When one member of the group shares their fears, despair or how utterly lost they feel without their loved one, others also open up more courageously. Of course, in order for this to happen there has to be a safe place to share. It is my responsibility to create this container by talking about the need to accept people where they are with nonjudgement. Once this safety has been established the sharing can go deep about their feelings and the experiences people are having.

Often in our groups someone will bravely share an experience of when they felt that their deceased loved one communicated with them. Initially they are hesitant to share and concerned about what the others will think. They often start their sharing by saying something very similar to what Dawn said to me. "I have never told this to anyone before, but . . ." Then they will go on to talk about an incredible encounter they have had with their loved one who has died or signs they feel they have received.

It takes courage to share these experiences, as those who have not had these types of experiences are often quick to judge or criticize. I myself had fear come up about writing this book, fear that I wouldn't be respected in my field if I shared these stories or that people would judge me. But after seventeen years of hearing stories from my hospice families and having these experiences personally—and for many years denying what I was hearing and seeing as being "illogical"— I have come to realize that the only rational thing to do is to believe.

It's fascinating to me how, when one person talks about an unusual experience they've had around the death of a loved one, others often want to share the experiences they've had. I see this time and again in my bereavement groups. As soon as one person breaks the ice with their story, several others then feel safe enough to share their own experiences. In reporting these commonalities, my hope is that it will give many others permission to share their special stories as well.

If you have had an unusual experience around your loved one's death, I encourage you to find someone you feel safe with and tell them about your experience. You may be surprised at how many others can relate to your story or have experiences of their own to share. If you aren't ready to tell your story, that's okay. I do want you to know this: You are not crazy, you are not alone, and such experiences are much more common than you know.

Questions to Dance With...

Write in detail about an unusual experiences or coincidences you or someone you know has had around the death of a loved one.

What was your first thought/reaction after having or hearing about these experiences?

What are your thoughts/feelings about sharing this experience or what you read here with others?

Guide *Me* Out of the *Pain*

Everybody needs beauty as well as bread, places to play in and pray in,
where nature may heal and give strength to body and soul.

~John Muir~

S HE WAS NOT EXPECTED TO live more than a few days. She was
widowed, childless, and living in a nursing home. That was all I knew
about Lucy the day that I met her. When I walked into her room
she was moaning loudly, struggling to breathe, and in obvious distress. I
ran for assistance. The nurse on duty, looking tired, barely acknowledged
me. When I pushed for help she informed me, "The medication is on its
way but there is nothing we can do for her until it arrives."

Frustrated, I rushed back down the hallway, noticing the pungent smell
of urine in the air just before I entered Lucy's sterile, colorless room. My
heart was racing as I sat down on the cold metal chair next to her hospital
bed. Unsure of how I could help her, I introduced myself to Lucy. Her
eyes were squeezed tightly shut, her body was tense and rigid, and she
did not respond. I wondered if she was even aware that I was there. It
appeared that she was using all her energy and focus to deal with her pain.

Whenever I start working with a patient, I try to take a moment to quiet my mind and connect with my higher self for inner guidance. For me, part of connecting with that energy happens through prayer, and when I pray at the bedside of my patients I am often amazed at what happens next. So I said a silent prayer for Lucy, hoping for some sense of how I could help her.

After praying, I felt guided to ask her this question: "Lucy, do you like to go to the beach?" I was surprised when she whispered a faint "yes," her eyes still squeezed tightly shut. Instinctively, I stood up and leaned over the bed's hard metal railing. I carefully took her cold hand in one of mine and wrapped my other arm over the top of her head, as if I were cradling an infant. Then I began whispering in her ear. "Lucy, I want you to imagine you are at the beach. You can feel the sunlight on your face, and you feel it warming your whole body. Feel the soft, wet sand between your toes. Notice the light ocean breeze as it gently caresses your skin. Notice how beautiful the water looks as the sunlight dances on the waves."

At first, Lucy held my hand very tightly. But as she listened, I felt her body relax. Her grip loosened and her breath slowed. She opened her eyes but had a faraway look in them. She kept saying, "Beautiful, how beautiful." I continued to guide her with my words, "Can you feel the cool water lapping around your ankles? Oh! And the sunset is so magnificent— the sky is ablaze in pinks and purples."

As often happens when I am with people who are dying, I become so connected to the present moment that nothing else matters. And so it was while I was with Lucy. Unaware of the passage of time, I simply stayed with her, holding her hand and giving her my full attention. By the time her medication arrived she was relaxed, her breathing calm. She expressed her heartfelt appreciation to me, this stranger who had entered into her world at such a challenging time. When I left, Lucy was sleeping peacefully. She died later that night. I knew so little about her but felt blessed by this holy encounter.

Suffering is Optional

This was another example to me of how powerful our minds are. I believe that before I came into Lucy's room and started working with her, she had been fixated on the pain. I've learned that whatever we give our attention to increases. Lucy suffered because her pain was her only focus. And then, with a shift in focus, her pain subsided.

We have this power available to us anytime we are suffering. It can be about physical or emotional pain. The next time you have the experience of suffering (you could be feeling depressed, anxious or angry), stop and just notice what you are focusing on. More than likely you are focusing on that which causes you pain. For example, if you just had a relationship end, you might be rehashing that last conversation, or you may be focusing on being alone this holiday season. Notice where your attention is and then consciously shift your focus onto what is working in your life, or what you are grateful for. You will notice that just by shifting your focus you will have immediate relief.

With Lucy, the focus went from her internal pain to the more global, felt-sense experience of being on the beach, hearing my words, and feeling my touch. This sweet encounter was a great reminder for me because I, too, can find myself focused on what is not working in my life. If you are not able to stop thinking about that which is causing you pain, try listening to a guided visualization online, or journal to unload your negative thoughts and resolve them by writing about all that you have to be grateful for in your present reality.

The simple act of writing down what you are grateful for can be a powerful way to shift your focus. When I was a bereavement counselor I worked with a lot of men and women who had lost their spouses. Naturally, they were heavily immersed in their grief, with their primary focus on their loss. I often made the recommendation that they start a gratitude journal. Although it may have sounded ridiculous to them at the time in light of the tremendous loss they have experienced, I knew that it would help them to shift their focus.

Initially, it was quite difficult for many of them to find anything they felt grateful for. But there was a simple self-predictive beauty in knowing that their homework was to write down five new things every night. They began looking for things to write down. As a result, they started noticing when the cashier in the grocery store smiled at them, or when a fellow driver let them in during rush-hour traffic. Slowly, their focus shifted. The end result was that they no longer focused on their pain or loss anywhere near as often as they had before. They also came to see how many things there were to be grateful for.

You don't have to be grieving to benefit from keeping a gratitude journal. It can be as simple as writing down five new things that you are grateful for every night before you go to bed. Try it for six weeks and watch for the inevitable shift in your level of joy.

Questions to Dance With...

Is there something in your life that has been causing you pain? It can be physical or emotional pain. Write about it in detail.

What are some of the thoughts you have about this situation?

List five things you are grateful for about this situation. Go ahead. I invite you to dig deep.

Permission

If you love someone, you must be prepared to set them free.

~ Paulo Coelho ~

S OMETIMES WHAT LOOKS LIKE SUFFERING may be holding on. We found that to be the case with Edward. He had been close to death for days and seemed to really be struggling in his dying process. This can often look like physical pain— moaning, labored breathing and restlessness. Once any physical causes have been ruled out, we begin exploring what else could be causing the struggle. Are they waiting to say goodbye to someone? If they have seen everyone they would have wanted to see, could they be holding on out of concern for their loved ones? Are they worried about how loved ones will cope once they are gone?

Over the years I have found that people who are dying from terminal illnesses have the ability to "hold on" (at least to a point). They seem to be able to "put off" and control the moment when they finally let go. I have seen family members do a vigil around the bedside of a patient for weeks, never leaving them alone. Then in that one moment when the patient is left alone, they let go. I have also seen patients who have not eaten food or accepted liquids for many days, sometimes even weeks. Yet they still remain alive, with hospice staff questioning how they can still be breathing. Then when that last missing family member makes it to the patient's bedside, the person dies— sometimes mere moments after that family member walks through the door. And sometimes, people need "permission" to die.

In Edward's case, once it was determined that there was no physical reason for his pain, we began to explore possible emotional reasons for the struggle he was in. He was an only child, widowed, with one daughter, Joanna, and three grandchildren. The hospice nurse and I both talked to Edward's daughter about why he might be holding on. She said that he had seen his grandchildren, friends and extended family. She did not think there was anyone else he was waiting to see. As we talked to her, she shared about how close she and her father had been through the years.

I mentioned earlier, in Amy's story, that giving permission for someone to die is not always what patients need to hear, but there are certainly times when people do need permission. After hearing about Joanna's close relationship with her father, I asked her if she had given her dad permission to go. She looked uncomfortable as I brought this up. I explained that sometimes people hold on because they are concerned about how their loved ones will do without them. She admitted sheepishly that she had actually been begging her father not to leave her. She said, "That's exactly what he would do. I was Daddy's little girl, and he has always put my needs first. If he had the ability to hold on for me, he would." I encouraged her to trust her instincts as to what he might need to hear, as it is different for every patient. After we talked she said adamantly, "I have no doubt that he needs to know it's okay for him to go and that I am going to be alright."

She went to her father's side and began telling him what a great father he had been to her and how much she loved him. She said that she knew he was tired and that, although she was going to miss him terribly, it was okay for him to go. She assured him that she would be okay. We all saw him visibly relax. As she talked, the lines on his forehead smoothed and his breathing slowed. I left the room to give Edward and his daughter Joanna time to be alone.

About thirty minutes later I was walking back down the hall towards Edward's room to check on them, when a chill ran down my spine. I felt the hair on my arms stand up and suddenly the air felt heavy. At that moment, Joanna stepped out of her father's room and said, "I think he's gone." I had actually had the thought, "I think I felt him go by."

By this time in my career I had been with many people as they left their bodies. When I was with someone as they died, I often had the same physical response that I experienced in that hallway the day Edward died. I always thought my physical reaction was due to an emotional response from witnessing this sacred event. But this was the first time it had happened before I knew the patient had died. After this very tangible experience, I came to believe that I was actually feeling the departing energy of the dying person as they were leaving their body.

Freedom Occurs in Letting Go

I was reminded of the importance of freeing another as I witnessed Joanna letting go of her father. She stopped begging him to stay, as she realized that keeping him trapped in a body that was not serving him was not the loving thing to do. Sometimes the most loving thing we can do for another is to let them go.

I was once in a relationship with a man who loved me deeply. It was a whirlwind romance and within a few months we were living together. But soon after moving in together it became apparent to me that we were not a good match. As this became clear to me, I began to try to ease my way out of this relationship. I was so afraid that I would harm him by ending the relationship that I allowed things to be in limbo for months.

During this time he was laid off from his job. Although I ended our romantic relationship, I stayed in the apartment and supported him for several months longer, thinking that

I was helping him. When I finally realized that I was feeling resentful and trapped by this relationship, I knew I needed to move. I left, feeling incredibly guilty about abandoning him as I did so. What I discovered instead was that as soon as I moved out and let go of the relationship, he soared. He found a job within a couple of weeks and stepped back into his power, reclaiming his life. He was also free to find a relationship with someone who could love him in a way that I couldn't.

I knew that Joanna had done this with her father, releasing him from the bondage of their father-daughter relationship. When she released him, she gave him permission to soar, to be free, to move on to his next adventure. In the moment that she freed him, she also freed herself, as she had felt tortured watching him linger. This experience and my own personal experience demonstrated so clearly to me that when we free others, we free ourselves.

Questions to Dance With...

What or who are you holding onto that is no longer serving you? Write about it in detail.

What is it that keeps you engaged with this person or situation? What are you getting or how are you benefiting?

What concerns do you have about releasing this situation or person?

How might your life be different if you let go?

Ultimate Sacrifice

True love is selfless. It is prepared to sacrifice.

~Sadu Vaswani~

OFTENTIMES MY PATIENTS NEED HELP letting go into death. Some may need "permission," as Edward did, to hear that it's okay for them to go. Others may need the right circumstances to help them let go. The latter was the case with my patient Margaret.

It was a Friday morning and I was notified that I had a new patient. Unable to reach her family by phone, I decided to stop by the nursing home where she was living to meet her. When I walked into Margaret's room, she was surrounded by her four middle-aged daughters. Her tiny body was propped up with pillows as she lay in her hospital bed looking small and frail, yet regal. She was talking softly to her daughters. They were all leaning in, straining to hear what she had to say, not wanting to miss a word.

I felt like I had entered into another time, as if I were witness to an ancient ritual of the elder wise woman imparting words of wisdom to the younger women of the tribe, each one of whom was listening intently.

81

I waited, allowing her to complete her thoughts with her daughters before introducing myself. I walked over to Margaret and leaned over the rail of her hospital bed. She looked me in the eye, smiling, as I told her that I was a social worker from hospice. I explained that I had come to support her and her family. She took my hand and thanked me in a whisper. She then closed her eyes, took a deep breath and exhaled with a sigh. I felt her hand go limp in mine. I stood over her for a moment and then realized that she had not taken another breath. I didn't say anything for a moment or two as I wanted to be sure, and then I told her daughters. "I think she's gone."

I was stunned. I had never had a patient die in this way before. I actually had this crazy thought for a split second, "I hope they don't think I did something to her!" She didn't die in the typical way that many of our hospice patients die. She didn't linger, she didn't go into a coma-like state. Margaret was interacting with her family and me one moment and gone the next.

After they recovered from the initial shock of her death, her daughters told me that it would be just like their mother to let go when she knew they would have support. Because I had said I was there to support her daughters, they felt that it was my assurances that had given her permission to let go. Margaret had courageously released her concern for her daughters and let go, trusting that they would have the help they needed.

As it turned out, her leap of faith was a big one and an honorable one. Margaret, you see, had just come on hospice service the day before. There had been no time for her and her family to prepare for her immediate death, much less to plan final arrangements. But Margaret's trust was not misplaced.

My training allowed me to gracefully step in. I started calling mortuaries to get quotes and helped arrange for someone to come and pick their mother up. As I did the legwork for the final arrangements, the daughters were able to say their final goodbyes in peace, unencumbered for the moment by all those details. As they continued to sit with their mother and witness her body's transformation in death, it helped them accept the reality that she had died. It is this act of witnessing the final breath and the withdrawal of the life force of a loved one that can bring much needed closure to the family members.

Elizabeth Kubler Ross, author of numerous best-selling books on death and dying, once said that, in her work with dying children, she was surprised by how indifferent she felt toward the body once the child had died. She came to the realization that her "indifference" was a natural response to the fact that the life force of the individual was no longer there. I have had this experience with my patients as well. There is a tangible shift in energy that occurs when the life force withdraws from the body.

Of course, it is a different experience for family members whose loved one has left their body, precisely because they are "connected" to the body in so many ways. For Margaret's daughters, this was the body that had given birth to them, nursed them, disciplined them and comforted them. Her face was the face of the unconditional love and acceptance they had known since infancy. Theirs was a deep emotional connection to her body that I did not have.

Having said that, I would also like to offer another way to "frame" the death experience. This reframing has been one of hospice's greatest gifts to me. The precious human body is a vehicle, a lovely and complex shell that houses the life force. When the life force withdraws from its body shell it becomes like the empty cocoon that is left after the butterfly has emerged. There is no reason for us to remain attached to the cocoon because we know that the butterfly that was housed there is now flying free.

Let Love Decide

It is not unusual for people to wait for a particular situation to let go. I have heard the families of my hospice patients say things like, "I was alone all day with my husband, and then the neighbor stopped by to check on us. As soon as he arrived my husband died. I think my husband wanted to know someone was there to support me before he let go."

In Margaret's case, I was reminded of how strong a parent's love can be. To all appearances, she could have gone on for days longer. But she saw an opportunity for her children to be taken care of and chose to exit. Again and again I am privileged to witness the amazing human Spirit during this incredibly challenging time. I have repeatedly been moved by the generosity, courage and sacrifice my patients make for their loved ones.

We are bombarded in the news by so much violence, hatred and negativity. I have gotten to the point where I rarely choose to watch the news, as I don't believe it accurately depicts what's happening in the world. The reality I see is that there is a lot of love and courage in this world. I witness it every day in hospice. So many people are willing to sacrifice for their loved ones or fight death so they can get one more glimpse of their lover's face. And I have the privilege of witnessing these acts of love.

This display of the human spirit is unfortunately not considered to be "newsworthy"! But I want to vouch for the fact that it is incredibly moving and beautiful to witness. I can attest that it is the years I have spent in hospice that have renewed my once-shattered faith in humanity. It is my hope that what you read here is helping prepare the way for you to experience the fullness of the humanizing and renewing power of death.

Questions to Dance With...

What decisions or actions have you made as a result of your love for another?

How did that feel?

Describe an experience where someone gave freely to you out of love.

How did that make you feel?

Existential Musings

Come, come, whoever you are, wonderer, worshipper, lover of leaving.
It doesn't matter. Ours is not a caravan of despair. Come, even if you
have broken your vow a thousand times. Come, yet again, come, come.

~ Rumi ~

A N EXISTENTIAL CRISIS IS DEFINED as the moment at which an individual questions the very foundation of their life— whether this life has meaning, purpose, or value. My hospice patients are often engaged in this exploration at the end of their lives. Each person I work with is unique, and they bring all of their life experiences to their deathbed. If someone has major unresolved issues, part of the work they need to do to prepare for death is to come to terms with these issues.

I have worked with many men who had war experiences that they had never talked about. Seventy years later, as they are facing their deaths, they find themselves needing to process these experiences. But war, of course, isn't the only issue that comes up for men when they are dying.

Frank was haunted by other memories from long ago. Frank was an 87-year-old Asian man dying of lung cancer. He was a private man who was used to being in charge. Whenever I visited he would immediately dismiss his caregiver and meet with me alone. He seemed to be on a mission to get his affairs in order before his death, and he was "all business" when talking about his dying. He not only wanted to get his financial affairs in order, but he also informed me that he needed to take care of his spiritual affairs.

Frank was a soft-spoken man who had kind eyes, but whenever I looked into them I saw tremendous pain. I met with Frank on a weekly basis. Initially he was guarded with me, but after a while he began to open up. He shared that he had come to the end of his life struggling with regrets from the past. His past haunted him, and he looked back on it with shame.

Over time, he shared more openly about his disappointment in love. His wife had divorced him, and he had only a distant relationship with his children. They had all moved out of state years ago and rarely called or visited him. He had felt driven to work hard, and so he was not around much when his children were growing up. He felt that he had let them down. Now he felt it was too late to make amends.

He told me that his children knew about his prognosis but were too busy to visit. I encouraged him to share his regrets with them, but he was not comfortable doing this. I attempted to persuade him, but he made it clear that he was not willing. So, I backed off, not wanting him to shut down to me.

One of the challenges of being a social worker can be honoring others' right to self-determination, especially when you firmly believe that an action could be beneficial to them or their family. I have learned to surrender my will and allow people to follow their own guidance, even if I don't always agree with their choices. It's their journey, and I need to respect that.

I don't think Frank had ever talked to anyone about the things he was telling me. But I believe it was because he was met with acceptance and love whenever he shared with me that he began to open up even more.

On several occasions he told me that he had some unfinished business with God. I encouraged him to meet with our chaplain, a priest, or a monk. Frank had been exposed to the Buddhist faith in his younger years, but he was raised Catholic. He had left the Catholic Church years before, disheartened with religion. When offered a spiritual counselor, he would respond by saying, "Maybe, when it gets closer to the end." I told him that we don't always know when the end is coming, but he felt sure that he would know.

Late one Tuesday afternoon I went to Frank's home for our weekly visit. As soon as I arrived, his caregiver quickly left the house. Frank informed me that he had asked her to leave. I felt a sense of urgency from him that I hadn't felt before. When I asked him what was going on, he told me that he felt the cancer growing quickly. He didn't feel he had much time left. Then he said something that took me totally off guard. He said, "I want you to take my confession." I explained that I was not trained to take confessions but that I could get him a priest that day. He said adamantly, "No, I don't want a priest, I want you."

Although I felt ill-equipped to take a confession, I knew that he felt strongly about this. I have learned over the years that if someone feels they don't have much time left (even if they don't look like they are at the very end of their life) I need to listen to them. So, I agreed to hear his confession. Before beginning, I prayed silently to be used in that moment to provide Frank with whatever he needed to come to peace with his past.

When Frank began his confession, the pain of his past came flooding forth. For over seventy-five years he had guarded these painful secrets, and they had impacted his relationship with his wife, his children, and himself. He had never talked about what had happened to him until now, the very end of his life. He shared painful memories of himself as a seven-year-old boy repeatedly molested by a beloved uncle. He went on to share memories of himself as the 12-year-old boy who in turn molested his little sister. His story was full of pain and shame.

He cut ties with his sister due to the shame he felt whenever he saw her. And regretted not asking for her forgiveness before her death. He had distanced himself from his own children for fear he might do something to harm them. He talked and cried, and as he did, years of regret and burden were released. He searched my face for judgment, but there was only love. I felt great love and compassion for this eighty-seven-year-old "little boy." When he finished, I offered a prayer about forgiveness and love. My words were guided; they seemed to come *through* me but not *from* me.

As Frank cried, he softened. The desperate urgency that I had seen in his face when I first arrived was gone. Afterwards he told me that he felt much lighter. It was hard to imagine that he had carried this shame for nearly seventy-five years.

Frank died a week after "unburdening" himself. I felt tremendous sadness after he died. Not because he had died (that was inevitable), but because he had wasted so many years protecting his secrets. Even in the end he couldn't face sharing what he viewed as his shameful past with his family.

What might his life and his relationships have been like had he "released himself" from his painful story years ago? The wall that he had erected to protect himself kept everyone else at a distance and prevented him from developing close, loving relationships. Saddest of all, Frank never really lived his life because he used all of his energy to protect himself and to shield others.

Take Off the Armor

Frank reminded me of how often we make decisions about the world at a very young age and then unconsciously live from that place from there on out. We learn from our early painful experiences in childhood to put up emotional walls to protect ourselves from any possibility of being hurt again. We walk through our lives with this armor on, often adding to it over time. But the walls we build and armor ourselves with do not protect us. In fact, it is just the opposite: These walls can destroy our lives.

True, our armor may keep us from feeling pain. But it also keeps us from feeling love, joy, and happiness. It is an illusion that the walls and armor protect us. My hope in sharing Frank's story is that it will give others permission to stop putting their core energy into protecting themselves. And instead will support them in tearing the walls down by taking the armor off and releasing the hold of the stories about why they have to wear it. I invite you to begin to walk bravely among the living. See yourself with compassion. Allow others to see you. Give yourself permission to open up and experience the magnificence of life.

Everybody carries burdens. That is just part of the human condition. But let's take a look at what they really are and see if we can't lighten our loads a little. As you saw in Frank's story, carrying these "burdens" by holding tightly to the pain and trauma of the old stories can have a profoundly negative impact on our relationships. It mercilessly saps our energy and compels us to keep our armor on, and our walls up.

I invite you to spend a little time with the next series of questions to do a little "deconstruction work" in order to free yourself from anything that may be hindering you in this way. I wonder how Frank's life might have been different had he had the self-compassion to see how he was holding himself back.

Questions to Dance With...

Write about one experience from your life that may have resulted in you wanting to protect yourself. What is one story you continue to tell from a childhood trauma?

How did you respond to this trauma? Did you build walls? Or make decisions about life or people? Elaborate.

How has this experience and the decisions you made impacted your life and your relationships?

Guru or Priest

Have patience with everything that remains
unsolved in your heart. Live in the question.

~ Rainer Maria Rilke ~

LTHOUGH FRANK HAD NOT BEEN willing to see a priest, he
still needed the ritual of confession to come to peace with his
past before he could let go. He was clear that one of the things
he personally needed was to make peace with God before he died. But
sometimes our patients aren't consciously aware of what they need to find
peace at the end of life. Visha was one of those patients.

Visha was not his given name but the name he received while visiting an
ashram in India. He followed a guru and referred to him as his Master. He
prayed to him several times a day and kept his picture above his bed in the
nursing home. A frail, anxious man, he told me the only thing that calmed
him was his meditation. When I talked to him about being on hospice
he made it clear that he did not want to talk about dying. Consequently,
when I would meet with him he shared stories of his travels and his time
in India. Sometimes he would read passages to me from his guru's book.
He was strong in his faith.

Oftentimes when people are aware of their terminal diagnosis, they desire to make amends in order to heal past relationships. They have a need to forgive and be forgiven, so they take care of unfinished business. Through the process of reconciling their past they often grow more peaceful as the end grows nearer. This was not Visha's process. He seemed to get more and more anxious as his body grew weaker. In Kathleen Dowling Singh's book, *The Grace in Dying*, she talks about the three stages that people often go through as they die. Those stages are chaos, surrender, and transcendence. Visha appeared to be stuck in the stage of chaos, which often involves a great deal of anxiety.

As he felt his body slowly shutting down, he appeared to get even more paranoid and anxious. An underlying anger that he could not (or would not) verbalize showed up in his interactions with his family, the staff at the nursing home, and the hospice staff. He refused to talk about what was happening to him and became defensive when anyone brought it up.

As his paranoia grew, he told me that he did not want me looking into his eyes because he knew that I have looked into many people's eyes as they were dying, and he did not want to receive that kind of energy. My initial reaction to his request was to think he was a little eccentric. But the truth is that there are unseen forces at play in our lives at all times, most of which we are unaware of. I sat quietly to ponder his request. I realized that, although I have often felt the energy of the life force of a patient when it leaves their body, many others in the room with me have felt nothing. So who was I to say that there wasn't some validity to his concern? At the very least, I knew that I needed to honor his request.

This turned out to be a real challenge for me. As someone who prides herself on being able to make a deep connection with people, often through eye contact, this request from Visha really threw me for a loop. I didn't know where to place my gaze, and I found myself feeling very disconnected from him. But this was his journey, and I firmly believed that my job was to respect it. So, difficult as it was, I made a point of not looking into his eyes.

His children longed to talk to their father about his dying, but he would have nothing to do with them when they tried to have these conversations. The only thing he ever told them was, "If my heart stops, leave it alone." Making it clear that he did not want his life to be extended or aggressive measures to be taken. But he stood firm in his refusal to voice his feelings about dying.

The day came when Visha became unresponsive. He entered into the coma-like state that often occurs in the last days of life. But with Visha there was an added uncharacteristic restlessness. He moaned constantly, his body rigid. He appeared to be fighting to stay alive.

Because Visha was struggling, the hospice doctor and nurses began the process of ruling out any physical symptoms that might have been causing his discomfort. It was determined that everything that could be done to ease his physical pain was being done. I explored what else could be causing the struggle, asking the family, "Is there anyone your father might want to see that he hasn't seen?" His sons shared that he had only a handful of friends, and they felt he had seen everyone he would want to see. I asked if there was anyone he had unresolved issues with or any special dates coming up he might be holding on for. They could think of none. For days we sat by feeling powerless as we watched him continue to fight against death. It was painful to witness his struggle. His family had all given him permission to go and encouraged him to let go. And still, he hung on.

After more than a week of watching this struggle, the chaplain and I met with Visha's three sons who had been doing vigil around his bed. They shared about his colorful past and talked about his childhood. As they talked, I became aware of the constant moaning in the background. I realized the sound that had been distressing to all of us had now become commonplace.

His sons shared stories and laughed, and Visha, moaning louder, made his presence known throughout the conversation. As we talked one of his sons mentioned that he was raised in a strict Catholic home and attended Catholic school until he graduated from high school. They shared that when he was in his twenties he went on a spiritual quest that resulted in him rejecting the teachings he was raised with. He had never set foot in a Catholic Church again. Visha had never shared this part of his life with us.

The chaplain asked if they thought it was possible that a part of his struggle might be concern about not having last rites? He explained that this is often an important ritual for many of our Catholic patients at the end of their lives. They said they couldn't imagine that he would want this as he had denounced Catholicism years ago. But because they were tired of watching their father suffer and felt that all other possibilities had been exhausted, they were willing to try anything.

The chaplain assigned to work with Visha happened to be a Catholic priest. Because of his role as a chaplain he did not always share his denomination with families unless he felt it was something that would serve them. His focus was on always meeting people wherever they were spiritually. He let the family know that he could administer last rites. We lit candles and dimmed the lights in order to prepare for this holy ceremony. Visha had always enjoyed visits from our chaplain. He was a kind, gentle man.

After preparing the room we all circled around Visha, holding hands. The chaplain set the tone through prayer and then administered the sacrament. Tears were flowing freely down all our faces as we encircled him in love. As the chaplain said his final prayer, something amazing happened. Within moments of receiving the ritual anointing, he stopped struggling, his breathing calmed, his tense body finally relaxed. He looked peaceful for the first time. His sons were thrilled. They joked that he wanted to make sure he was "covered" spiritually. Within an hour of receiving the last rites Visha took his last breath.

Re-examine Past Beliefs

I think the greatest gift I received from Visha was the lesson that, any time I'm struggling in life, it can be beneficial to revisit my past to see if there is some unconscious belief holding me back. Experts say that our formative years are between the ages of one and five. During these years we develop deep-seated beliefs that are imbedded in our psyche, beliefs that were introduced to us before we could make rational decisions. They become a part of who we are without our even being aware of them. These include spiritual teachings.

We make many decisions about life based on our childhood experiences and then live from those decisions. We may decide that God is an angry, vengeful entity to be avoided. We may decide that other people are not safe because we have been hurt. Our clever human psyche even goes one big step further. Once we make a core decision, it starts gathering evidence to build a case that proves that we are right.

In a workshop I attended years ago a man shared about a decision he had made when he was an adolescent. He was convinced that his mother didn't love him because she had never said the words, "I love you." He went on to share more "proof" that his mother didn't love him. He told us that he had been in a serious car accident and for three months his mother sat at his bedside every day, not once telling him that she loved him. He was so entrenched in the story of "my mother doesn't love me" that he couldn't see what an act of love it was for his mother to be at his bedside every day for three months.

We often make decisions like this early on in life and then go on to live out our lives patterned on those decisions. Even when there is ample evidence that we are wrong, we can't see it because we are entrenched in our story. As this man shared, the other participants could see what he could not: that his mother loved him. He was looking through the filter of "my mother doesn't love me." There's a good ending to this story. Over that weekend he was able to free himself and his mother from that story that he had lived with for so long.

During that same weekend I also uncovered core beliefs that I had been carrying since I was six years old. Mine were sourced in "the day that my parents left me behind." We were visiting my grandmother that day, and when it was time to go home they loaded up our old Ford station wagon. My five siblings and I were all under the age of seven so, needless to say, my parents had their hands full. They didn't realize until they were almost an hour down the road that I was not in the car. This happened years before the advent of cell phones, so there was no way my grandmother could reach them.

Of course, I didn't understand any of this. All I knew was that I had been forgotten—that my parents had forgotten me. From that traumatic experience my six-year-old psyche made two very weighty core decisions about life: (1) that people could not be trusted, and (2) that I was not important. And *boy*, did I ever buy into those decisions hook, line and sinker!

During the weekend workshop I became aware of how, throughout my life, I had been gathering evidence to confirm those two decisions, including dating several unfaithful men. Of course, there were many times in my life when people had honored their word or let me know that I mattered, but that was not where my attention went for many years of my life. Instead, I looked for evidence that people were not trustworthy and that I wasn't important. You better believe that I made note of it every time there was an experience that confirmed my theory!

That workshop broke open my great defensive wall and helped me see how much those decisions I had made at the innocent age of six were keeping me from living the joyful and connected life I desired. So, here again in hospice, I got to see clearly how peoples' thoughts and beliefs had impacted their lives and were now influencing their deaths. I began to reexamine my negative ways of viewing the world. I knew that, if my life was going to work for me, I needed to shift my thinking and my focus. I made a commitment to seek out books and seminars that would help me find new ways of thinking and being in the world.

In Visha's case, he had been raised to believe that you need to receive the last rites before you die to ensure that you will get into heaven. Although he later came to reject those teachings, somewhere deep in his psyche that belief still lingered as a core belief. (If your core belief was that you will go to hell or purgatory if you don't receive the last rites before you die, then you can bet you are going to fight death until you get them!) Even if you aren't consciously aware of a core belief based on a decision made in childhood, the belief still lives within you. I suspect that is why Visha could not verbalize what his anxiety was about. His core belief was rooted in his subconscious mind, and Visha's conscious mind was simply not aware that he was still carrying that belief.

Though Visha had not been one of my easiest patients, I became very grateful to him. He gave me such a strong and helpful reminder to take a good hard look at my own beliefs to make sure that I was not still living life from my six-year-old's perspective.

I encourage you take a look at your own core beliefs. I know . . . that sounds arduous, even scary. But, believe me, the rewards for taking a mature inventory of those very old and often impaired beliefs are greater than you can possibly imagine! Oftentimes these core beliefs are our greatest "blind spots." If you don't feel like your life is flowing as it should and are unsure why, there are hundreds of personal growth workshops that can help guide you to look a little deeper and, at last, see what you haven't been seeing. The beauty is that the blocks we can't see are often the blocks that others can clearly see, so recognize that we are surrounded by plenty of support to let go of that which no longer serves us.

Questions to Dance With...

Can you remember the first time in your life as a child when you felt that you were not safe? Or that you had been deeply hurt or traumatized? Describe this memory.

What decisions about life, people or yourself did you make at that moment? (You might not have been conscious of it until now).

How has your response or the decision you made impacted your life?

If you are ready to release this story, what is a "worthy" story or belief you can replace it with? For example, if you made a decision that you were not lovable, are you willing now to replace this story with a new one that says, "I am lovable"?

Between Worlds

The most beautiful thing we can experience is the
mysterious. It is the source of all true art and science.

~ Albert Einstein ~

Expanded Awareness

A FEW YEARS INTO WORKING WITH the dying I became aware of an interesting phenomenon. When patients are dying slowly, as many hospice patients are, they can enter into this realm that I refer to as "between worlds." The line between their life and the spirit world seems to soften and become more permeable. They seem to have an expanded awareness of what is happening around them. During this time people's eyes often become brighter. They seem to be lit up from the inside. Often they have experiences that cannot be explained by logic. Rose was one of my patients who dwelt between worlds.

She was stone deaf. I literally had to yell for her to hear anything at all. Even then, she would only get little snippets of what I was trying to say. One Tuesday morning I stopped by to see how she and her family were coping. She had children visiting from out of state, so we decided to have a family meeting. Rose lived in this magnificent 3,000 square foot Victorian style house. We met in the main living room, which was on the other side of the house from Rose's room. Rose was sleeping most of the time in those days, so she did not join us in the meeting.

Her children talked about how they could not believe she was still alive. We discussed the reasons that she might be holding on. I went through the questions I often ask when people are lingering long after their predicted demise. I asked if there was anyone in the family she still might be waiting to see. They all agreed that she had seen everyone.

In fact, Rose had called each of her family members in to see her, and during these meetings she had spoken openly to them about her dying. They all felt they had said their goodbyes and had given her permission to go whenever her heart called her to move on. I asked them if there was any significant event coming up such as the birth of a grandchild, a wedding, a birthday or anniversary or any other significant event. They got excited when they realized that her wedding anniversary was coming up in a few weeks. After much discussion, her family members agreed that they had solved a mystery: She must have been waiting for her anniversary.

At the end of my visit I went back to the other side of the house to say goodbye to Rose. Her son Allen was with me. We were both taken by surprise when we walked into her room and she exclaimed, "I'm not holding on for my wedding anniversary." Then she proceeded to repeat verbatim the things we had just discussed.

None of the other family members had been in her room since our meeting. When we stepped out of her room I asked Allen if there was a monitor in his mother's room. He said there wasn't. That means that, even if Rose's hearing had been good (which it really wasn't) there is no way that she could have overheard our conversation. Rose needed assistance to even get out of her bed, so I knew she could not have left her room. Physically, there was no way Rose could have heard our conversation, and yet, she had.

Deathbed Visions

Another common occurrence for my patients when they are close to death is that they may start seeing their deceased loved ones, spiritual beings, even deceased pets. This is commonly referred to as a deathbed vision.

My first experience with a deathbed vision was when I was an intern. I was assigned a patient named Kathy, who was living in a nursing home. I visited her on a weekly basis. As I began to explore her feelings about dying, she let me know that she considered herself an agnostic and didn't really have any beliefs about the afterlife. I could relate to Kathy, as we had similar beliefs at the time, both of us unsure whether there was life after death. Needless to say, after many long conversations about her doubts about life after death, I was very surprised one afternoon when I was meeting with Kathy, and she leaned over and whispered, "Do you see her?" gesturing toward the foot of her bed. There was no one else in the room, so I asked her to tell me what she was seeing. She said, "There's an angel at the end of my bed." She was calm and appeared lucid as she went on to describe the angel in a white flowing gown with huge white wings. I asked her if it scared her to see an angel and she said, "No, I feel so much love from her."

As soon as I left Kathy's room I called my supervisor to let her know that Kathy was having hallucinations. I asked her if Kathy was on some medication that could be causing these hallucinations. My supervisor responded, "No Cheryl. In fact, she went off all her medications when she came on service." I asked, "Well, does she have a history of mental illness that could be causing these hallucinations?" She chuckled and said, "No Cheryl, she doesn't have a mental illness." She went on to explain that this was a common experience for people who were dying. Although she said it was common for the dying to have these experiences, it was certainly not a common experience for me. I was sure there had to be some reasonable explanation.

I continued to visit Kathy on a regular basis, and frequently during our visits Kathy talked about the angel being present. She was always very matter-of-fact and calm about it. A few weeks before she died, she also shared that she saw her mom (who had been dead for twenty years) standing outside her nursing home window looking in. I asked her why she thought her mom was there and she said, "She's waiting for me." As a new hospice social worker, I continued to be very skeptical, thinking that this is just wishful thinking at this difficult time in her life. But Kathy, who started out just as skeptical as I was, died convinced that she was going to be with her mother and the angels.

Since then I have heard about hundreds of experiences like these and been with many patients as they are having these experiences. I learned from Kathy the importance of staying open and getting curious when someone is having an experience.

I had another lovely experience while visiting my 80-year-old patient Tracy. She, too, was on very little medication and was lucid and clear thinking. During my visit with her I noticed that she kept looking past me and smiling. Twice, I actually turned around, thinking someone must have walked into the room. I soon realized that she was seeing someone that I couldn't. I asked, "What do you see, Tracy?" She smiled and replied, "It's my husband. He's waiting for me." Her husband had been dead for two years. With tears in her eyes she went on to say, "He can't wait to dance with me again!"

Not every patient who has these experiences sees someone they recognize. My patient Hector kept telling me about a man who would come and stand at the foot of his bed. He described him wearing a beige trench coat and a fedora hat. I actually went to the nurse's station to see if a man had been visiting Hector, but they weren't aware of anyone.

It wasn't until I was sitting with him one afternoon and he said, "Well, here he is again!" that I realized his visitor was coming from the other side. I later talked to his daughter about this visitor. She, too, had been present when he was seeing his visitor. She shared that Hector used to work for the FBI. She said that she had old pictures of her dad with his fellow FBI agents, and they all dressed just like the man her dad kept seeing at the foot of his bed. She felt certain that her dad was seeing someone he had known during that chapter of his life.

Interestingly, as I have been with people having these experiences, I've noticed a pattern in their gaze at these times. My patients will often be looking up toward the right corner of the ceiling. Some will have full-on conversations with these invisible beings (at least invisible to me), or they will wave or smile or reach for them. For the most part these visitations seem to bring patients peace. It can be distressing to patients when well-meaning family members, who are in the room at the time say, "Mom (Dad), there is no one there; you are seeing things." Hearing this can be disconcerting for patients, as the visions they are having are very real to them.

What patients say when they are having these visions covers quite a spectrum. I have heard patients tell these invisible guests that they are not ready to go yet. I've heard other patients carry on their half of a complete conversation. Sometimes it is apparent that they are looking at something I cannot see, but they are unable to articulate who or what they are seeing. I had a bereavement client share that their mother had been in a coma for days, totally unresponsive, but at the time of her death her eyes shot open and she sat up with her arms outstretched to the ceiling, with a look that they described as ecstasy. She then fell back into the bed and died.

I initially tried to explain away these experiences as side effects of medication, but I have had many patients on little to no medication who still have these experiences. Because of the many mystical things that I have heard about and experienced around death, I have come to believe that it is possible they actually are seeing images from the other side.

The Thinning Veil

Another level to this expanded awareness, as the veil between this world and the next gets thinner, is an awareness of what is happening "on the other side." An example of this is my patient Basil, who had dementia. His wife June had died while we were working with him. His family had chosen not to tell him, as they felt that with his dementia he might forget again and then have to be retold and relive the sad news. His family went as far as not to tell the nursing home staff to ensure that Basil didn't overhear them talking about his wife's death. June had lived in a nursing home herself and hadn't been able to visit her husband for several months due to her own health issues.

For a year prior to her death Basil repeated the same prayer over and over again, always using the same words: "Lord, guide me through the valley of death, Lord be with me now." A few days after June died, I went to see Basil and was surprised to hear a change in his prayer. He had abruptly changed the wording of his prayer to "June, guide me through the valley of death. June be with me now." I talked to his daughter after my visit and she said that he started praying the new prayer the day after June's death. She was shocked by this and said that no one had told Basil that his beloved June had died, but somehow, he knew.

Similarly, I had patient named Lee whose wife went into the hospital while he was on our service. While she was in the hospital, Lee died. Again, because of her fragile state, the family chose not to tell her about her husband's death. But the day after his death she announced to the family, "Dad has moved upstairs and I am going to be joining him tomorrow." They were stunned that she seemed to know that he had died and even more stunned when she died the next day.

Transcending the Mind

I have also witnessed patients transform in the last few days of their lives. I have seen, on several occasions, dementia patients who had been confused for years have a period of clarity at the end of their lives. Suddenly they recognize family members they haven't been able to recognize for years.

One of the most unusual experiences of transcending the mind occurred with my patient Sean. He was probably one of the most difficult patients I have ever worked with, as well as one of the most rewarding. He was in his late 70s, had been diagnosed with paranoid schizophrenia in his mid-thirties, and was now faced with a diagnosis of terminal lung cancer after years of heavy smoking to calm his nerves. After that diagnosis he experienced an increasing number of anxiety attacks.

I worked with Sean for several months prior to his death. I learned that, prior to the onset of his mental health issues, he had traveled overseas and done missionary work. He now lived on disability and had moved in with his elderly uncle. According to Sean, "They look out for each other."

Sean could be clear thinking one day and angry and paranoid the next. His thoughts were often scattered. It was difficult to carry on a conversation with Sean without him becoming defensive or suspicious. I feared that as he declined, his anger and anxiety would increase, making it difficult for his elderly uncle to manage him at home. While working with Sean I often asked to connect to my guidance to know how to best serve him. I prayed that he might find peace at the end of his life, as he had spent so many years in turmoil.

Something unexpected and, dare I say, even "magical" happened as he got closer to the end of his life. It seemed that the paranoid ideas and the anger began to fall away. It honestly felt like his mental illness was just lifted away, and his essence began to shine brighter and brighter. In his last weeks he gained clarity he hadn't had for the entire nine months that I had known him.

Sean told me in great detail about his years of travel and missionary work. Those memories seemed to have gotten lost or jumbled as his mental illness had taken over. As his body grew weaker his memories and thoughts became clearer. He shared his missionary stories proudly, as if to say, "I did make a difference on this Earth!" I watched as his conflicted relationship with his uncle softened. Sean's eyes began to shine more brightly, and the anxiety he had dealt with for years was replaced with a serenity that was glorious to witness.

He spent his last days reminiscing and expressing appreciation and love to those around him. Naturally, his uncle was having a difficult time letting go. Because of this, Sean did not get the peaceful death that I had hoped he would have. The night his body began to shut down Sean's breathing became shallow and labored. Instead of calling hospice when his breathing changed, his uncle panicked and called 911. He died in route to the hospital.

His uncle later told me that Sean was calling out for me when the ambulance took him. At first this made me uncomfortable. I was concerned that I had crossed some professional boundary that I shouldn't have. But when I thought about it I knew that, because of his mental health issues and the unpredictable behaviors that came with it, Sean had lost most of his friendships. His mother, who had died ten years earlier, had been his biggest support. Over the last nine months of his life I had sat with him, listening without judgment to his stories of failures, successes, joys, and heartbreak. I had soothed him when he became anxious. I had become someone he saw as a friend or a mother figure. From what Sean had told me, it had been a long time since he'd had a friend. I felt honored to be viewed in this light by him.

We are More Than Our Bodies

As my experiences with the other side have multiplied it has become clear to me that we are so much more than the flesh and bones we identify with. I have heard spiritual teachers say that we are "spiritual beings having a human experience." This makes sense to me, all the more so because it is supported by the mountains of evidence I am exposed to in my work.

It is comforting to me to know that we can transcend the life issues and circumstances we find ourselves in while living in this body. The knowledge that we humans are, first and foremost, spiritual beings comforts me and impacts the way I live my life. For one thing, I don't feel like I have to take life so seriously anymore. I can relax and know that everything that is happening is by divine appointment.

We can't know why Sean's experience included mental illness, but I am grateful that he was finally able to have clarity about his contributions and accomplishments as a missionary. Sean's life was, for me, another example of how unique each of our human/spiritual experiences is. As I've delved more into spiritual teachings I have a strong sense that whatever it is that is guiding our lives is loving. I don't claim to know what it is, but I do believe that there is a higher power and that we have a higher purpose than we can see from the perspective of our mundane, everyday lives. I trust that when difficult things happen in my life, they are happening for my soul's expansion.

My father asked me once, when we were talking about my sister Shelly, "If God exists then why has Shelly had to suffer all these years with health issues when so many people have prayed for her to be healed?" I pondered this question for a while. As I looked at my sister's life, it was really clear to me that it was the graceful and positive way my sister dealt with her health challenges that inspired so many others, including myself. Shelly was a light shining brightly in the darkness for others who struggled. She has been an example of what is possible in life.

As my beliefs have shifted over the years, I have come to believe that we come to this Earth for the further evolution of our souls. I suspect that brave souls like my sister volunteer to have these experiences for their own evolution, as well as to inspire others to reach for the highest expression of theirs.

I am sharing my opinion here, but I invite you to take the time to ponder what feels right for you. I know that we can all access guidance and wisdom within ourselves. I know that it does not serve us to blindly follow anyone else's opinion of what is right or wrong or what our purpose is on this Earth. Go within . . . enter the stillness . . . listen . . . and trust what comes.

As you review the next set of questions I invite you to explore, perhaps a little more deeply than you have before, what you truly believe. Trust your heart.

Questions to Dance With...

What are your beliefs about having a soul?

Do you believe that there is a part of us that lives on after we die? (Say more about this.)

What is your sense of why people go through challenging situations in life?

Old Blue Eyes

Don't ask what the world needs. Ask what makes you come alive, and go do it. Because what the world needs is people who have come alive.

~ Howard Thurman ~

TOM WAS A 60-YEAR-OLD MAN who was dying from an inoperable brain tumor. The hospice nurse informed me that Tom had tumors throughout his brain. Due to the location of the tumors he was experiencing paralysis. He had also lost his abilities to talk and to write. He was divorced and his only son lived out of state. There was no one to care for him so he was living in a nursing home.

The first thing I noticed when I met Tom was his beautiful blue eyes. They had such depth. He seemed unsure of me as I introduced myself. As I sat next to him, feeling uncertain of how I could connect with him, I became aware of two nurses in the corner of the room discussing Tom's most recent bowel movement as if he weren't present. I took Tom's hand, leaned toward him and said, "Don't you just love it when people talk about you as if you aren't even here?" He rolled his eyes and squeezed my hand. A look of relief washed over his face as I made it clear that I knew he was still very much alive and present in this body that no longer worked for him.

I told him that I knew he'd lost his ability to speak and write. Realizing that he could squeeze my hand, I told him that we could still communicate. I asked him to squeeze my hand once for yes and twice for no. When I asked if he understood this he squeezed my hand once. So began our conversation.

Wanting to determine how much he knew about his condition I asked, "Have the doctors talked to you about your medical condition?" One squeeze, "Yes." Do you know about the tumors? One squeeze, "Yes." Through my questioning and his responses, I was able to determine that he knew he had a terminal diagnosis and wasn't expected to live much longer. He maintained eye contact with me throughout our conversation, fully present. Sensing that he was starting to trust me, I began to explore his feelings about dying. This is the conversation that ensued:

Cheryl: Have you thought about dying Tom?

Tom: (one squeeze) Yes.

Cheryl: Are you afraid?

Tom: Yes.

Cheryl: Are you afraid of the process of dying?

Tom: (two squeezes) No.

Cheryl: Are you afraid you will suffer?

Tom: No.

Cheryl: Do you worry about what will happen to you after you die?

Tom: Yes.

Cheryl: Do you have a belief about what happens to people after they die?

Tom: No.

Cheryl: Do you think people have a soul?

Tom: (There was no squeeze.)

Cheryl: You don't know whether we have a soul?

Tom: Yes.

Cheryl: So now that you are faced with death you are curious about what might happen?

Tom: Yes.

Cheryl: Would you like to talk to one of our chaplains about this?

Tom: (There was no squeeze.)

Cheryl: Are you uncomfortable with structured religion?

Tom: Yes.

Cheryl: Are you afraid they will try to push their beliefs on you?

Tom: Yes.

Cheryl: (I explained that our hospice chaplains are very respectful of our patients' spiritual perspectives.) Would you like to think about talking with one of our chaplains?

Tom: Yes.

As I sat with Tom, I felt unsure of how I could help him explore what lay ahead for him. I sat in silence for a moment, connecting with my inner guidance. Then I remembered a truly wonderful tool that might be able to help him: the small and very poignant book and CD set entitled *Graceful Passages: A Companion for Living and Dying,* created by Michael Stillwater and Gary Remal Malkin. It is designed to companion people through their dying process, as well as "for anyone who is interested in exploring their personal mortality." The set includes two CDs. On the first CD, "The Messages," twelve spiritual teachers from different traditions around the world share their beliefs about death, dying and life through music and spoken word. The second CD, "The Music," is the music alone from the first CD without the narrations.

When I told Tom about *Graceful Passages*, he let me know that he would like to hear it. Although I had been told that Tom could not communicate, in that first meeting we had a meaningful conversation. I felt honored that he had shared so much with me and was willing to entrust me with his fears.

On my next visit with Tom I brought the *Graceful Passages* CD with narration and music. Before I played it, I checked with him again to make sure he still wanted to listen. I told him that I would stay with him as it played so that it could be stopped at any time. I started the CD and sat down next to Tom. The hauntingly beautiful music began and then we heard the resonant voice of Lew Epstein say this:

"No one has ever prepared us for this experience.
We think it's the end - no.
It's another beginning,
another beginning...."

That day we listened to the entire ninety-minute CD. Tom listened intently to each spiritual teacher. I would check in with him after each one to make sure he wanted to continue. When we came to the end of the CD I asked him if he had found it helpful. He gave my hand a very firm squeeze "Yes."

I wasn't sure which part of the CD had been the most meaningful to Tom. Was it the Native American woman Jyoti talking about the Great Mother or Ram Dass speaking about preparing to die by identifying with the soul? Or was it one or more of the other spiritual teachers? Although each narrator had come from a different spiritual background, all the messages held the common thread of hope and love.

By the end of that day's visit Tom seemed truly peaceful. I again offered to have a hospice chaplain come in to speak with him. This time he said yes. I don't know what Tom had heard that day that had brought him peace, but something had clearly shifted for him. He was able to communicate to me that he no longer felt so afraid.

I visited Tom regularly over the next few weeks. One day I arrived with a fun surprise for him. His son, who lived out of state, had informed me that Tom loved Frank Sinatra. Tom's face lit up when I showed him what I had brought him. I put on the CD, then I sat next to Tom and took his hand so that he could communicate with me. But that day, instead of talking, we danced.

Tom held my hand, moving it back and forth to the music, maintaining eye contact with me throughout the dance. Those beautiful blue eyes of his twinkled with delight. At the end of our visit I bowed and thanked Tom for the dance. His thanked me with his eyes and a squeeze of my hand.

I didn't know then that this would be my last visit with Tom. Later that same week he died peacefully in his sleep. My heart hoped that he had found beautiful things waiting for him on the other side of his death, and I felt so blessed to have shared that final dance with Tom.

Never Stop Dancing

I was moved by Tom's authenticity and his honesty. He faced his death with courage and curiosity even in the face of his inability to communicate. In order to support him under these incredibly challenging circumstances, for which I had had no real preparation, I had to trust my instincts, that "something greater" that my hospice experiences had taught me to connect with and rely upon.

As I had with previous patients, I once again experienced the near magical power that is accessible in the moments of "presence" when we are being fully present with one another. Tom demonstrated to me how deeply and purely we can communicate with each other without saying a word. Although Tom was severely limited in his "verbal" communication to giving my hand a Yes or No squeeze, he communicated volumes to me through his eyes. Through our focused gaze I was given the privilege of meeting and becoming one with "the Being" who was named Tom.

Perhaps words could never have communicated what we shared that day through our eyes alone. That profound experience with Tom reawakened me to how much joy we can experience in the simple acts of humanity.

The most important lesson I learned from Tom was that you are never too sick, too old, or too incapacitated to dance. I will always cherish that special soul dance I had with him, hand in hand, during our last visit. I'm sure that Tom would be in 100 percent agreement with me on this: Never stop dancing or doing whatever it is that brings you joy!

Questions to Dance With...

What brings you joy?

What stops you from having more pleasure in your life?

How can you bring more of what lights you up into your life?

Sins of the Son

*The heart of a mother is a deep abyss at the bottom
of which you will always discover forgiveness.*

~Honoré de Balzac~

LTHOUGH SOMETIMES A PATIENT NEEDS to revisit old teachings
(Visha) or figure out what they believe (Tom), there are also
times when patients need to redefine what they believe in order
to find peace at the end of their lives.

Chandra was a quiet, timid African American woman who was dying of
end-stage heart disease. She looked frail and weak as she lay wrapped in
a black and red flannel blanket, gripping her pink rosary beads. I felt her
deep sadness during our first conversation. She had five children: Four
were living, her son Tyrell had died by suicide a few years before. One
of her daughters told me that she was not surprised that her mother was
dying from heart issues. According to her, Chandra had not been the same
since her son's death. She felt her mother was dying from a broken heart.

During my visits with Chandra she spent most of the time talking about
Tyrell. He was twenty-eight years old when he killed himself. Her
youngest son, she always considered him "her baby." She said he was

always sensitive and caring, and that they had a special bond. There was a wide age difference between him and her other children, so she had been able to devote more time to him while he was growing up. It was clear that she had not worked through her considerable grief. Our time was spent processing her heartbreak and the terrible guilt that often comes when a family member commits suicide. She talked about what a good boy he was and how much she missed him.

While Chandra was growing weaker, she shared with me that she was not afraid of dying. But she was deeply troubled by the teachings of her faith. She explained that the Catholic Church she attends teaches that suicide is a sin and that you cannot go to heaven if you take your own life. She wept as she talked about her despair in thinking that she would never see her son again. I asked her if she might like to have one of our chaplains come out and talk to her. I explained that we have a very loving and open-minded Catholic priest who might be able to help her. Reluctantly, Chandra agreed to talk with him.

I am not a Catholic, but I wanted to respect her beliefs. So I tried to be especially careful about what I said to her. I could see that she was really struggling with these issues and I knew that if she did not find some resolution, she would probably have a rough passing. So I talked to our chaplain right after my visit with Chandra. He shared with me that he did not agree with the stance that many in the Catholic Church had taken regarding suicide. I felt he was the perfect person for Chandra to have this conversation with.

Unfortunately, when he went out to see Chandra, she was unresponsive. Her family reported that she was fading in and out. She would be unresponsive one day and able to carry on a conversation the next. He was not able to talk to her about her concerns. We felt that she had only days to live, but once again we were witnessing the restlessness that often comes when the patient is dealing with unresolved issues.

The next day I stopped by to check on Chandra. To my surprise she was awake. Though she was in a severely weakened state, she was able to talk with me. Soon after I arrived, our conversation again turned to Tyrell, who was weighing heavily on her heart. She again shared how much she missed him. Although I had hoped that the chaplain would be the one to talk to Chandra about her son's suicide, at this point I knew that I needed to take this opportunity to carry the conversation further with her. I didn't want to risk her falling back into that unresponsive state.

You learn quickly in hospice that you cannot wait for the "ideal situation" to arise. The present moment is the opportunity we have—and there may not be another opportunity. I said a silent prayer to be connected with the wisdom within me and to be guided in this important conversation with Chandra.

I asked her to tell me about the God she believed in. She shared that to her God was like a loving father. She felt he was kind and compassionate. She talked about feeling God around her often and felt so much love when she had these experiences. I said to her, "Wow, what a beautiful image. So you think that God is like a loving parent?" She replied, "Yes." "In other words, God loves you the way you loved Tyrell?" She responded strongly, "Yes." It was then that I said, "I think that anyone who takes their own life must be in such tremendous pain." She looked surprised by this sudden topic change but agreed.

I asked her next, "Can you imagine ever turning your back on Tyrell when he was hurting so much that he wanted to die?" She answered firmly, "No, never." I agreed, responding, "I can't imagine any loving parent turning their back on their child when they were in so much pain." She nodded in agreement. I paused for a moment and then asked "So, why would God?" Without hesitation, she responded. "He wouldn't." Her eyes lit up and she said again with conviction, "He wouldn't!"

It seemed that she had had the truth that she needed to hear inside of herself all along. The God she loved so much would never abandon a child in pain. There was a deep *knowing* that came over Chandra. Her usually meek demeanor changed as she claimed this truth. She had come to her own conclusion about God and how he would treat his beloved children.

By the end of our conversation, the tension and burden I had seen in her face were washed away. She looked serene as we said our goodbyes.

Before that conversation, as Chandra had been dancing her final dance, the overwhelming anxiety she was experiencing had made her unsure of her footwork. But after that conversation she soon completed her final dance with ease and grace, slipping away tranquilly in the night with her four children around her. Her family felt that she was at peace at the end.

My hope for Chandra was that as she crossed over she was greeted by Tyrell's outstretched arms. I believe that she was.

Truth is Within You

I was reminded from my visit with Chandra that the truth we often seek through our churches and spiritual teachers is within us. Although I asked Chandra questions that may have helped her to find her answers, her responses came from deep within. And I know that my questions were guided from deep within me.

Although I am a spiritual person, I have often struggled with structured religion, believing that religion, for the most part, is man attempting to control man through interpretations of spiritual teachings. Spirituality to me is a person's individual connection to source energy/God/the Universe (or whatever name you want to give it) that we all have access to.

When I first started on a spiritual path, I attended all kinds of churches and spiritual centers. I soon became amazed by the diversity in and disparity between interpretations of the Bible within the sects of Christianity that I was being exposed to— and my exposure was far from comprehensive.

In my graduate program I gave a presentation on women and religion. While doing research to prepare for this talk, I found many examples of how interpretations of scriptures had been twisted and tweaked or how phrases that implied God could be feminine had been excised. One example was the word

El Shaddai, which was translated to mean a "God in High Places." Although this was one definition of the word, there was another definition that was not included and that was "God with breasts." As I researched this topic I began to question how so many churches could say that their interpretation of scripture was "the right one."

My time with Chandra reminded me to question the beliefs that come to me from the outside and to seek answers from within. Whether we listen to it or not, I believe that we all have internal guidance. For me that still, small voice within is the voice of God. It is what has guided me into and through my work with the dying, as well as into writing this book. Here, the life lesson for me has been to trust my own internal guidance rather than to look outside of myself for answers.

I am involved in a spiritual community that I chose because, for the most part, what they teach resonates with me and it feels good to be there. But when something new is being introduced I always step back and ask, "Does this fit for me?" I trust that I will be guided and led to the right path for me and that you will be led to the right path for you. I believe that there are as many paths as there are people. We are spiritual beings having a human experience, each on our own unique spiritual journey.

I have learned from every one of my patients as they have struggled and tried to make sense of their lives. Sometimes their religious beliefs have been comforting to them, and sometimes those beliefs (current or imprinted long ago) have caused a lot of turmoil at the end of their lives (Visha and Chandra).

I have come to see that although there are many beautiful spiritual teachings, we were never meant to follow them blindly. We have the truth within us and one way to access this truth is to get still and listen. We tend to make it so complicated, but it's really very simple. There are threads of truth in all religions. Unfortunately, humanity easily gets caught up in fighting over the details, complicating what is meant to be simple and beautiful. There is one statement in the Bible that says everything that needs to be said: "God is Love" (John 4:8). If we wholeheartedly tune into what love is and live from that place, then we could have a world that works for everyone. If we all lived from love, we would only know peace. In love there is no prejudice, no hatred, no war.

As you go through the next series of questions I invite you to trust your guidance and your instincts. Do not be afraid to question anything. We were given the gifts of curiosity and intuition for a reason. We all have the ability to tap into truth—and when we do, we know without a doubt that we have.

Questions to Dance With...

Do you believe in a God or a Higher Power? If so, write about that. If not, say what you do believe in and write about that.

Are there mainstream religious or spiritual beliefs or teachings that don't resonate with you? What are they, and where do you disagree with them?

Are there teachings from childhood that you have been carrying that no longer serve you?

Golden Light

Faith is the strength by which a shattered
world shall emerge into the light.

~ Helen Keller ~

MY FIRST MEETING WITH KAREN was brief. She kicked me out of her room as soon as I stepped in. She was anxious and agitated, as many people diagnosed with dementia can be. I went back a few days later to see if I would have any better luck connecting with her.

When I arrived at her room in the nursing home, I found Karen to be close to death. Her eyes were half open and had a faraway look in them. She was taking quick, shallow breaths with periods of apnea. The nurse examined her and confirmed that her blood pressure was very low and that there were other physical indicators that her body was beginning to shut down. Her husband was called and informed of her condition.

After Karen's husband David, arrived I began to prepare him for what he might see in the next few hours. He looked panicked and insisted that he could not stay. He explained that he was a veteran and had been in World War II. He went on to say that he had held many of his buddies in his

127

arms as they died and knew he couldn't handle watching his wife take her last breath. Tearful, he leaned over Karen and gently kissed her cheek, saying his goodbyes, and then he left. Karen became restless as soon as her husband left. I stayed with her, wanting to provide reassurance.

I said a silent prayer, asking for the words to console her. During David's brief visit he told me that he had never talked to his wife about his war experiences as he didn't want to burden her. I shared with her how touched I was by the tender way David had interacted with her, telling her that it was apparent how much he loved her. I told her that I believed his need to leave was because of his love for her, that he cared so much for her he couldn't bear to watch her go.

Although she was in an unresponsive state, I continued to talk to Karen. I told her about the bereavement services that hospice offers to family members after the death of their loved ones, and I assured her that David would have support if he was willing to accept it. I shared with her from my experience as a grief counselor that one of the beautiful things about grief is that it opens people up. It gives them an opportunity to heal not only their current loss, but unhealed wounds from the past as well. I suggested that this could be a real opportunity for David to heal the trauma of his war experience. This seemed to calm her.

As I sat with Karen she had bouts of choking as her lungs filled with fluid in spite of the medication she had been given. When this happened she would become agitated. I knew that Karen was getting close to the end of her life. I began looking around her room for clues as to what might bring her comfort. I noticed that she had many plaques and awards from her volunteer work for the Methodist church on display. I inferred from these that her religious background was a traditional Christian one. I used this as a cue to engage her spirituality, hoping to soothe or at least lessen her agitation.

When she got panicky or anxious I would ask her to picture the God that she loved so much wrapping his arms around her, holding her as a parent holds their child. I asked her to imagine what God might say to her as he held her. I told her that he must be proud of her for the way she had served him all these years. I could see that the things I was saying to Karen appeared to be comforting to her because her body relaxed and softened and her breathing slowed. (When using guided visualization with dying patients, I pay close attention to their reactions to help me know if I am on the right track.)

Karen was in a coma-like state, but I assumed that she could hear me. I have had it confirmed many times in the past that a dying person who is in an unresponsive state can still be aware of what is happening around them and what's being said. I have seen people come out of these states and narrate the full story of what had taken place. It's part of the expanded awareness. They are able to say who talked to them and what was said, as well as who talked about them as if they weren't present. I'm always mindful of this as I interact with people at the end of their lives, always assuming that they hear and understand me. Even if they have dementia, I assume that on some level they understand. The responses I've gotten over the years have confirmed this belief.

As the hours passed I talked to Karen about the family pictures on her wall and the awards that were framed. Noticing that Karen's church bulletin from the Sunday service was on her night stand, I decided to re-enact this service. I recited the Lord's Prayer, "Our father who art in heaven . . ." hoping that these familiar words would comfort her, I sang the first verse of *Amazing Grace* (all that I could remember) which was also part of the service. After ending the makeshift service with prayer, I used the rose-scented lotion on her night stand to gently massage her hands, arms, and feet. I felt as if I were anointing her.

Once Karen seemed relaxed and peaceful, I sat with her in the sacred silence, sensing that she was getting very close to the end. Sometimes the most important thing we can do with someone as they're dying is to just be a loving presence in the room. As I sat next to her, I noticed a golden light illuminating her face. I looked around the room trying to figure out where the light was coming from. The only lamp in the room was the one next to her bed and it was off. The overhead lights were off and the curtains were closed. I couldn't see any place in the room where the light could be coming from. I thought, "Well, that's strange," and then shrugged it off. A few moments later Karen drew her last breath.

It is a surreal experience to sit with someone in the last hours of their life. I felt blessed to have midwifed Karen through her dying process. I left the nursing home that night and stopped at the grocery store on my way home. I felt like I was walking in an otherworldly fog, thinking, "Wow, I have the strangest job in the world." Walking down the aisles among the shoppers in the brightly-lit store, I had this thought, "I was just sitting with someone as they died and now I'm grocery shopping. Wow!" I felt the urge to yell out, "Karen died!" I knew that it didn't matter to the people in the store but it mattered to me.

A few days after my experience with Karen I received a gift from the universe. I was making a condolence call to Theresa, the daughter of one of my other patients whose mother had died a few days earlier. As we talked she shared with me that her family had had the most beautiful experience as their mother passed. She said, "We saw my mom's spirit leave her body." I asked curiously, "What did that look like?" What she said next gave me goose bumps. "Her face lit up with this beautiful golden light moments before she passed. It was so incredible." I was instantly taken back to Karen's room, seeing her face as it lit up, and having no explanation for that golden light. As Theresa shared her experience of her mother's transformation, I knew that I had been privileged to witness Karen's.

I felt that it was no coincidence that Theresa shared this experience with me. I have learned that there are often things that happen in the weeks leading up to a death, and often for months following a death, that can't be explained by the rational mind. On the other hand, I have so often observed that when we humans fail to come up with an explanation for an "unusual experience" we often try to rationalize it away by laying the blame on our grief, our imaginations, or our exhaustion.

I know in my heart that these experiences are as real as any others. Thanks to hospice, my mind and my life have been "retooled" to both accept and be enriched by such experiences. I firmly believe that by staying open to these experiences we are afforded a glimpse of divinity.

Give Others Your Undivided Attention

When I was trying to comfort Karen, I knew so little about her that I had to be fully present and attuned to her. I watched closely for her reactions as I made attempts to bring her comfort. It was very much a dance, as I adjusted what I was doing or saying based on her reaction. When I would see her relax or notice her breathing change to a slower pace, I knew we were in step and that I was on the right track. I have no doubt that I brought comfort to Karen that day. I felt deeply connected to her even though we had never had a conversation or interacted in any meaningful way before that day. Yet it was a powerful experience, a true honor, and a sweet benediction to be her dance partner in her final hours.

Every one of our personal relationships could expand exponentially and beautifully if we gave them this kind of undivided attention, letting everything else fall away. What would our relationships be like if we were fully present to those we love most? If we paid close attention to the other person's responses, moving with them rather than against them? This is the way we were always intended to be with each other in this dance of life.

We were meant to be connected, heart to heart. But in this age of technology, the quality of our interpersonal communication seems to have been shoved into the back seat in favor of putting quantity in the driver's seat. We always have a choice, and that is what I urge us all to remember. We can choose to shut off the television set, the cell phone, and our computers and practice "being" with each other without all the distraction.

It may be challenging at first, that I don't deny. (Distraction seems to have become the default "ambiance" of our lives.) Many people these days seem to be realizing what they've been giving up - and little by little choosing tranquility and simplicity over flash, dash and more noise. It is in the place of non-distraction where our minds and bodies can truly relax, where worthwhile conversations can happen, where our hearts can open to one another as well as ourselves. That is where we will foster the deep, rich connections we all long for. The best news is that we don't have to wait until someone is on their deathbed to connect in this way.

I challenge you to try non-distraction for a day— to be fully present with those you love. Unplug . . . be available . . . listen fully . . . and be aware of how your interaction is impacting other people. Engage in life in a meaningful way and be ready to be awed.

Questions to Dance With...

Describe a time in your life when you were fully present to another.

Who do you long to connect more deeply with?

Are there areas in your life where you know you are "distracting" yourself rather than fully engaging? (Pick one and describe it.)

What is one thing you can do right now to disconnect from distractions?

Dancing Queen

Silence becomes cowardice when occasion demands speaking
out the whole truth and acting accordingly.

~Mahatma Gandhi~

CRYSTAL HAD GROWN UP IN the arts. She loved to dance and had travelled around the world performing in a dance troupe for many years. She had worked with many famous stars and been deeply involved in the performing arts. In her later years when her body could no longer tolerate the demands of training as a professional dancer, Crystal taught dance to budding stars. She never married nor had children, focusing her time and energy on her true love, dance. She had a colorful past, and she loved talking about it as much as I enjoyed listening to her life adventures.

When I first met this 85-year-old woman, I would never have guessed that she had been a dancer for most of her life. She was overweight and unkempt and did not reflect the image I had of a professional dancer. The day I met her I said to her, "I heard you were a dancer." She responded angrily, "I *am* a dancer!" I stood corrected.

In my work I've noticed a pattern that elderly patients seem to fall into.

Those who have lived extravagant lives are either incredibly grateful or really pissed off at the end of their lives. Crystal was the latter. She was angry about her illness and her condition. She was used to being waited on and catered to. She could be quite short with hospice staff who came to care for her. She was upset if they did not jump when she said jump.

Honestly, I didn't like her much at the beginning. I disliked her entitled attitude and the way she talked down to me and my co-workers. But knowing that her behavior was not the whole story, I knew I needed to dig a little deeper. What I found underneath her anger did not surprise me. As with many other patients, Crystal was harboring a great deal of fear.

She did not believe in an afterlife. When I first met her we had a talk about dying. She made her pronouncement loud and clear: "When we die we become worm food, and that's it!" Over the years I have learned that those who believe in "this is all there is" are often beset by a lot of resistance and fear around their deaths. I attempted to help her to process her feelings. Crystal made it clear that she wanted nothing to do with examining her feelings or her beliefs.

Instead, I spent my time with her facilitating a review of her life, which seemed to bring her pleasure, as she reminisced about her varied experiences. Although she didn't want to talk about dying, she began to prepare for her death, ensuring that her affairs were in order, signing over bank accounts and real estate, and giving away possessions. Crystal also began making phone calls to those she was closest to, as well as those she needed to make amends with. She made a point of telling them what they meant to her, apologizing for any ways she may have wronged them, and saying her goodbyes.

In his book *The Four Things That Matter Most*, Dr. Ira Byock discusses what most people define as being the most important things to say before you die. They are "Thank you," "I forgive you," "Will you forgive me?" and "I love you." I truly doubt that Crystal had read this book, but she instinctually knew what she needed to do in order to prepare for her death and was doing it.

What I came to appreciate most about Crystal was the fact that I always knew where I stood with her. She spoke her mind freely, and she did not sugarcoat anything. I saw a strength in her that I felt was lacking in my own life, as I had spent much of my life people-pleasing and being the good girl. I found her honesty refreshing.

Crystal was only on hospice for a short time. Her cancer had grown rapidly, and she was soon in the transition phase of her dying. She stopped eating and drinking and became more withdrawn, spending much of her time sleeping. She no longer wanted to interact with her visitors. Soon, she only allowed those who were closest to her to be at her bedside. She remained in control of her circumstances as much as possible.

In the last few days of her life she began talking about her beloved dog, Tango, who had died years earlier. She said that she could see and feel him lying next to her. She talked about this matter-of-factly. It didn't seem to upset her nor make her question anything. It appeared to comfort her. Her family jokingly said that she loved that dog more than anyone. I found it intriguing that this woman who believed so strongly that there wasn't any existence after this life did not question the fact that her deceased dog was now keeping her company.

I talked to her sister Linda after her death. Linda shared that Crystal appeared to have struggled until the very end. She had fought sleep for several days, fearing that she would not wake up. During this time she repeatedly talked about Tango being with her. Linda confessed that although they had all been raised to believe there is nothing after this life, she found herself questioning this view after her experience with Crystal's death. She said that she could not believe that an "energy as big as her sister's" could be gone. Linda shared how Crystal would walk into a room and others would be drawn to her.

She was also fascinated by the fact that her sister was convinced that her dog Tango was with her in her last days. She said that other than her talk about Tango, she appeared to be clear in her thinking. She laughed, saying that by the time her sister died they were all convinced that Tango was in fact with her. She found this thought comforting. She said she intended to explore further the idea that we live on outside of these bodies. I let her know that this was a normal response to her sister's death, knowing firsthand how death can pique our curiosity about life after death.

Speak Your Truth

Crystal was a great example for me of someone who spoke honestly without hesitation. Although she could be harsh or abrupt at times, she demonstrated to me the power of speaking one's truth. I sat with her as she opened up to her family and freely shared with them where she had wronged them as well as where she had felt hurt or misunderstood. I suspect that Crystal had always been candid and straightforward in her communications, but I wondered if facing her death had motivated her to be even more vulnerable in her sharing. As she admitted her own hurts and wrongdoing, her relationships deepened before my eyes.

It is not uncommon for people to share more deeply at the end of their lives. A man once told me that the year after he had been given a terminal diagnosis had been one of the happiest years of his life. The reason? Because he didn't feel he had time for any "bullshit" (as he put it) and he would speak his mind. In that he found freedom.

Many times I have witnessed the power of a single honest conversation. My patients and their family members have healed personal relationships that had been strained for years when they have taken responsibility for their wrongs and offered forgiveness to those who had wronged them.

I had a friend share his experience of breaking the habit of people-pleasing. He said that when he started setting boundaries and being more honest with people he found that some people did not like him as much. But more people came to respect him. The truth is that when we conform to please others we aren't being ourselves anyway, and that means that what others think they "like" in us isn't even real. Personally, I would rather be respected for who I am than liked because of a façade I put on to please others.

For a moment, stop and think about the energy we are expending in how we show up in the world. It takes tremendous energy to be something we are not, yet it takes no effort to be ourselves. I know for myself when I was a young adult in the dating scene, I would present to a potential partner what I thought he wanted me to be rather than showing him who I really was. Feigning interest in things (like football) that I wasn't really interested in. Then feeling resentment because all we ever did was watch football! The resentment that comes when we attempt to please others and deny our needs is toxic. Many illnesses are a direct result of pushing down those feelings of resentment and anger.

Witnessing Crystal in her authentic expression was a reminder of how much strength there is in being ourselves and speaking our truth. And also of how much power we give away when we aren't honest about how we are feeling, or how someone's behaviors have impacted us. I have learned as I began to practice "the art of being myself" that it is important for me to let go of what I hoped the outcome will be.

We can't control how someone might react when we tell the truth, especially if they are used to us always saying yes (or watching football). There is definitely an adjustment period for those who are used to our cooperation. Be patient with them as you practice setting limits, speaking honestly and allowing yourself to be seen. Try not to take it personally if they have a hard time accepting the changes and the boundaries you set at first. They will adjust or fall away. Either way will benefit you in the long run.

Questions to Dance With...

Are there situations in your life where you are being less than authentic? Where are you saying "yes" when you want to say "no"? (Describe.)

What are your concerns about setting boundaries?

Is there anyone you are blaming for your current circumstances? If so, who and why?

Describe where you might have played a part in creating the situation. Remember there is freedom in taking responsibility where you can.

Creative Messages from Beyond

Those who don't believe in magic will never find it.

~Roald Dahl~

OVER THE YEARS I HAVE done a great deal of personal and spiritual growth work, and because of this and the experiences I've had, my awareness has expanded. I have found myself more open to the mysteries of life (and death), more open to the life "energies" that we carry, and more attuned to the passage of the spirit out of the body at death.

In addition, I have learned by experience that messages can be sent from beyond the grave. As I look back over the years of my hospice work, I can clearly see my evolution in becoming ever more open to these messages. Let me be the first to admit that in my early days in hospice I had no idea how to pay attention to these messages - much less that there was any such thing. I have had experiences that another person might shrug off as coincidence, but I have come to know that these synchronistic events are so much more. Of course, I have had the luxury of having multiple experiences, which does reinforce believing in the magic, and mystery, when events occur.

Where the Fern Grows

One such experience occurred while working with a bereavement client named Grace who had lost her husband of fifty years. She was devastated by Harry's death, as they had been inseparable in life. I was counseling her in her home and worked with her for nearly a year. She was having a number of experiences in which she could feel her husband's presence. She would talk about feeling him in the room. At other times she would feel his hands on her shoulders when she was sitting at her desk. She said that it felt so real that she would turn around, but there was no one there.

During one of our sessions Grace pointed to a big pot on her patio. She said that the plant that had been in the pot had died five years earlier, and what was left in the pot after they'd removed it was just hard, dried-up dirt. Nothing had grown in the pot for all those years. But a couple of weeks after her husband's death she noticed little green shoots pushing up through the dirt. This was amazing to her, as she had not been watering the pot, there had been no rain, and nothing had been planted there.

During the months that I counseled Grace we were both in awe of the gorgeous fern that came to life in that pot. By the time our bereavement counseling came to an end the pot was overflowing with the most lush and beautiful fern I've ever seen. Grace was convinced that her husband was responsible for this. Apparently, she had complained to him about the empty pot for years, but they had never taken the time to buy a new plant to put in it. To me, Grace's story was another reminder that life in its fullness simply carries on. We can notice it . . . or not. But I believe that when we are open to life in all its richness, our lives are blessed in ways beyond our imagining.

Here to Support You

Several times during our time together Grace had mentioned feeling her husband touch her. It was not uncommon for me to hear about these experiences in which my bereaved clients heard, felt, and sometimes saw their loved ones. I worked with a man named Shawn who had lived with his long-time girlfriend Charlotte. She had died suddenly of an aneurism.

He said she had been healthy and strong one day and gone the next. After she died, he said that he began having an odd experience.

Shawn said that Charlotte was a night owl. He always went to bed before she did and found it comforting when she would finally crawl into bed and snuggle up next to him. A few days after Charlotte's death Shawn said that he crawled into bed and shut the light off. As he lay there unable to sleep with thoughts of Charlotte filling his mind, he felt someone crawl into bed. Startled he jumped up, alarmed that someone had broken into the apartment the two of them had shared. When he turned on the bedside lamp no one was there. This occurred several days in a row. At first Shawn said, "I thought I was losing my mind." As time passed he became convinced that it was Charlotte's way of comforting him. He soon relaxed into the feeling of having her next to him and found it reassuring. He said that sensing her at his side was the only thing that got him through this tragedy.

Over the years I have heard many stories from my grieving clients in which they felt or sensed their loved one in the room. Sometimes they would hear their loved one calling to them, or see them briefly in a hallway. One of my clients shared that a few days after her son's death she was standing at the kitchen sink washing dishes and had this flood of emotion come over her. She said she felt overwhelmed by her grief as hot tears were streaming down her face when she felt a loving embrace. As she felt invisible arms wrap around her from behind she heard her son's voice in her ear saying, "I'm okay Mom, I'm okay." A sense of peace washed over her in that moment that she can still access when she thinks about this experience with her son.

Another example of this came from a dear friend of mine, Rebecca. She shared that a few years after her father Jack died, her son Mark had a life changing experience. Mark suffered from depression which intensified when his parents divorced. After the divorce, his grandfather Jack stepped in to help raise him. He became more of a father figure and was always there for Mark. They had grown very close, so naturally when Jack died he took it really hard. At the time of Jack's death Mark did not believe in afterlife; he tended to be more "intellectual" about things of this nature.

Three years after his grandfather's death, Mark called Rebecca and asked her to go for a walk on the beach. As they walked he said, "Something unbelievable happened to me last night." He paused for a moment and then blurted out, "Mom, I saw grandpa last night!" He went on to tell her, "I was lying in bed when I noticed that I had left the bathroom light on. I laid there for a while not wanting to get up but I knew the light would bother me if I didn't shut it if. Annoyed, I got out of bed and went down the hallway to the bathroom. When I turned the corner into the bathroom, I was shocked to see Grandpa Jack standing there. The bathroom light was not even on. The light I saw was coming from grandpa! He held out his arms to me and as we embraced I was engulfed in a field of love like I have never felt before. Then grandpa whispered in my ear, "Marc, I'm happy where I am." He held me for a few moments and then he was gone." He told his mom, "I know how crazy this sounds mom but he was there." He felt that his grandfather wanted him to experience the incredible love that he was experiencing on the other side. He said it was a love like he had never felt before.

Rebecca told me that this encounter transformed Marc's life. He was a self-confessed atheist prior to this experience but is now very involved in spiritual community. He is now convinced that there is life after death and that those who have passed on can reach out from beyond the grave. A few years after this experience, Marc's grandmother died. Because of his experience with his grandfather, he handled her death much differently. He expressed peace about her passing and about his own death someday.

Rebecca said that she never had an experience like this with her father after his passing. She believes he visited Marc because of their close relationship and the fact that he was really struggling after his death. She said, "I already had a strong belief about life after death which was soothing to me. Marc had no faith prior to this experience." Although she would have loved to see her father one more time the way Marc had she felt he needed it more.

Gifts from the Ocean

Not all messages from the grave are as earth-shattering as Marc's experience. Some are subtler, but even those can provide tremendous comfort. One such experience occurred one stormy Saturday afternoon. I was walking on the beach— my form of therapy after a particularly rough week. I had been working with a young father who died the day before. Hank was a thirty-two years old surfer who loved the beach life. He had frequently talked about his love of the ocean. His early morning surfing trips were his form of church. He told me once he felt closer to God when he was out on his board than he ever had in any church. When he died he left behind a nine-year-old daughter, Tiffany, and an eight-year-old son, Jacob. I had been assigned to provide counseling to him and his children. Hank's wife had left him and their children the year before. This compounded the loss of their dad, leaving them especially vulnerable.

I found myself immersed in thoughts about Tiffany and Jacob as I walked. My thinking ran very much along the lines of how unfair life had been to those two innocent children. It had given them so much to deal with at such a young age. I was concerned that this might be more than these two could bear and I hoped my support would make a difference.

Prior to Hank's death I had worked closely with him and his children, supporting them in having some difficult conversations about his terminal status. I encouraged Hank to write each of his children a letter about what they meant to him and about his hope for their futures. Writing these letters took tremendous effort on Hank's part, but I knew that his children would treasure these letters for the rest of their lives.

Deep in thought about the children, I practically tripped over two huge conch shells. When I stumbled across them my body responded immediately with goose bumps. As I picked up the two glistening shells, I sensed that it was no coincidence that I had found these two treasures while thinking about Hank's children. I immediately *knew* that it was a sign from Hank. I have now lived in Southern California for fourteen years and I had never come upon shells like the two I found that day (and never have since). A sense of peace washed over me when I picked them up and there was a deep knowing that life goes on. I knew at my core that his children were going to be okay. After all, they had Hank looking out for them.

And there were yet more surprises, serendipitous encounters and validations ahead of me. As I continued my work with hospice. I soon learned that nature wasn't the only vehicle those who have passed on used to reach out to the living. Over the years I have seen or heard countless other creative ways that the departed communicate with their loved ones.

Scooter Fun

Modern-day electronics appears to be another vehicle that is used extensively for communication from beyond the grave. I have heard any number of stories about TVs turning on when people aren't in the room, or the lights flickering. One woman shared that all through the Christmas season (a few months after her dad had died) her Christmas tree would turn on when no one was around. It appears that electricity and mechanical devices are a handy conduit for communication from the deceased. Sometimes this communication is very specific to the person who died and their loved ones. They leave clues to make it clear that the message is from them.

I worked with a woman who shared that prior to her husband's death he loved riding on his apple-red electric scooter. She would walk alongside him as he went around the neighborhood. He had a bell on his scooter and would ring it constantly, which embarrassed her because it would often startle people. They disagreed about this: He found it funny and she did not. She admitted that she would get annoyed with him when he rang that bell.

She went on to share that after her husband died, the bell on his scooter would ring every night at 11:45 when no one was anywhere near his scooter. She even asked her son to examine the scooter. He could find no plausible reason for the bell to go off. She went on to explain that 11:45 pm was the actual time of her husband's death. She came to believe that it was her husband letting her know that he was okay and that he was still with her.

Midnight Snack

Another one of my bereavement counseling clients, Carla, shared an experience she had about a month after her husband died. She woke up in the night and heard cupboards opening and closing. She had been hearing noises like this since her husband died and thought it was her imagination playing tricks on her at night as she adjusted to living alone.

On this one particular night the noises were louder and more startling. Carla called out and no one responded. She said that she lay there for a while, and hearing no more noises, thought that she must have been dreaming. Then she drifted off to sleep again.

Carla was the only one in the house at the time. When she got up the next morning she was shocked to see cereal spilled all over the kitchen counter and several cupboards she had closed the night before wide open. Initially, this frightened her and she walked cautiously through her fifth-floor condo in case the hungry burglar was still in her home. She said the chain was still on the front door and the door was locked. All the windows and sliding glass door that led out to her patio were also locked and her alarm system was on.

After a thorough investigation, Carla felt sure no one could have gotten in. She walked back into the kitchen and then, as she re-examined the mess in the kitchen, she had a moment of deja vu and began to laugh out loud. She said, "This was not the first time I had walked into my kitchen to find a mess like this." She went on to share that her husband used to get up in the middle of the night for a snack and always left a mess on the counter and the cupboards wide open. She said she rarely had disagreements with him, but when she did it was usually about his late-night behavior. Her fear turned to gratitude as she realized that it was the perfect way for him to let her know he was still around.

I was concerned for this elderly widow and questioned her more about this apparent incursion into her home. What if someone had broken in? She assured me that there was no way anyone could get into her house because she had a first-rate security system, and no one else had a key to her home. She was convinced that it was her husband paying her a visit in a way that only the two of them would understand. His midnight snacking had not been a small thing in their relationship. It had resulted in either frustrated arguments or playful banter between the two of them for more years than she cared to count.

Pink Cotton Balls

After years of hearing about the unusual experiences people have around the death of their loved ones, I wasn't surprised when my parents had an unusual experience of their own after my aunt Dorothy died.

A few years before Dorothy's death she turned 70, and my parents made the long drive from Nebraska to Phoenix, AZ to help her celebrate her birthday. She was thrilled that they had come so far. After spending a long weekend with her, they were getting ready to make the drive home. She walked them to the car and thanked them profusely for making the long trip. My dad who was turning seventy in a couple more years said jokingly, "Now I expect you to be at my 70th!" And she responded, "Oh, I'll be there!"

A year later Dorothy was diagnosed with colon cancer, which had already metastasized to her brain. At a certain point we heard that she wasn't faring well, so I drove to Arizona from California, my parents drove from Nebraska, and other close relatives also arrived to spend time with Dorothy. She knew that she didn't have long to live and began to go through her prized possessions soon after our arrival. One by one, she called us into her bedroom to give us a hand-picked treasure that she had carefully selected for each of us.

She gave me a mischievous-looking angel statue from her collection. She picked out a delicate heart necklace for one of my cousins, and then she called my mom into her bathroom. Dorothy held out her hand like an excited child as she placed my mother's special gift into her hand and closed her fingers over it. My mom slowly opened her hand and was surprised to see nothing but two pink cotton balls. She held the cotton balls to her heart and thanked Dorothy for her thoughtful gift, knowing full well that Dorothy had periods of confusion as a result of the cancer spreading throughout her brain.

Aunt Dorothy died a few weeks after our visit. A year later, my dad turned 70 and there was a big celebration for him at my sister Karen's home. After the party was over, my parents went to get into their car. When they opened their car doors they were shocked to see two pink cotton balls on the passenger seat.

Now, I've got to tell you . . . My father is a bigger skeptic than I ever was. He did his darnedest to try to figure out how the cotton balls got there. Their car had been locked and no one had had access to it. The last time they'd been in the car was earlier that day, and those pink cotton balls had not been there. As they discussed the mysterious appearance of cotton balls mom exclaimed, "I don't even have a clue where you'd go to buy pink cotton balls!" Then she began to weep, remembering the promise Dorothy had made to my dad a few years earlier. The next thing she said, with a huge smile on her face, was this: "She made it, Lee—she made it to your birthday party!"

My down-to-earth, skeptical parents were both convinced that those two pink cotton balls were a sign from Aunt Dorothy. I have to admit that I don't doubt that for a minute. I have seen and heard about far "stranger" things happening since I started my job as a hospice social worker. Honestly, every experience I have had or heard about has caused my fascination with life after death to grow.

Stay Open to the Magic

What beautiful reminders I have had of how important it is to keep an open mind. I've learned that it is when we remain open and aware that we have an opportunity to receive messages from beyond. They aren't something you can force, but if you pay attention to the coincidences that occur around the death of a loved one, you will become aware of the messages intended for you.

I have become aware that when I'm fully engaged with my surroundings, life events, or another person, I am much more likely to have a mystical experience. My guess is that they actually happen all the time, but we are so caught up in our thoughts and other distractions that we miss the magic and sacredness in each moment's unfolding.

I have had bereavement clients who were frustrated that they were not getting messages or signs from their loved ones. I suspect that the messages are always there. When we are immersed in our grief— fearful about how we are going to handle our futures or lost in thought about memories of our loved ones— we miss these signs. In order to be aware of these messages and then to truly receive them, we have to be fully present in the moment.

Recently, I was talking to a woman named Jessica who was giving me a manicure. She was curious about what I do. As we talked I shared some of the unusual experiences I have had. She told me that she had recently lost her dad and shared that, although she believed that it was possible to get messages from the grave and had hoped for a sign from her father, she never got any messages from him.

Jessica went on to tell me about all the synchronistic events that had occurred after her father died, which resulted in her buying property that she did not think she would ever be able to get (something her father really wanted for her). She shared all the signs that led her to this property. As she talked it became clear to her that these synchronistic events that had occurred *were* signs from her father.

She realized that she had had a preconceived notion of what she thought these signs should look like. Because she didn't recognize the things that were happening as "communication from her father," she had missed his communication altogether. She was delighted when she came to the realization that he had been helping her from his new vantage point. Jessica was humbled and grateful that he had been communicating with her all along.

The point is that the messages you receive might not look the way you expect them to. But if you remain open, staying connected to the present moment and aware of your surroundings you will see the magic. I myself was a skeptic for many years! But over the years I have heard and experienced so many astounding coincidences and jaw-dropping stories that I can no longer deny them.

Questions to Dance With...

Have you ever had an "unexplainable" experience at the time of someone's death or after someone died?

Describe any coincidences or synchronistic events that you have experienced around the death of a loved one (. . . or any other time, for that matter).

How did it feel when you received these messages or signs?

My Expansion

Fully Embracing the Gift of Life

Life shrinks or expands in proportion to one's courage.

~ Anaïs Nin ~

As I was writing *The Final Dance* I became aware of how *significantly* I had been changed by my hospice work. Reviewing the many experiences I've had and the insights I've received from my patients, I realized that everything in my life had shifted. All of these had been transformed: The way I viewed life, my beliefs about death and life after death, and the way I showed up in the world. I was no longer the disheartened, burnt out social worker who was ready to give up on humanity. Instead I found myself reveling in the magic and beauty of life. Rather than numbing myself out with alcohol, I wanted to feel it all. The pleasures, the joys, the pain— I didn't want to miss one single moment.

My desire to be "more present" in life had this result: I embarked on a journey of self-discovery. I began taking workshops and going to classes to expand and grow. This was not an easy path. I had to face my demons and take a good hard look at myself.

A couple of years after starting hospice work I attended a personal growth workshop in hopes that it would help me better understand myself. It was an act of faith to attend this workshop. The longer I worked with the dying the more willing I was to take risks.

I attended a friend's graduation from this program and was shocked when, one by one, people were getting up to share how the workshop had impacted them. I was surprised to hear story after story of participants who had healed things in their relationships, which often takes years of therapy. One man had brought his mother, whom he had not talked to for ten years. In one weekend he took responsibility for his part in how their relationship had played out. He asked for forgiveness, and he reconnected with his mother in a deep way.

I was moved as he brought her up to the front of the room and they both openly wept and embraced. As the participants shared, I heard story after story of healing. I heard them talk about feelings of freedom and lightness. I knew that I wanted some of that! So I signed up for the program, no longer content to just "get by" in life.

During the first weekend of the workshop I felt nervous, wondering what I had gotten myself into. I looked around the room at all these well-dressed, professional-looking people. Off to my right I noticed a beautiful woman with bleached blonde hair, acrylic nails, and enhanced breasts. She was dressed in a colorful, sexy dress that made her stand out in the crowd. I wondered what I could possibly have in common with this flashy woman. I proceeded to pass judgment on her and many of the other workshop participants. Wow, I'd plunged headlong into a confounding realization: It was easy for me to see past my patients' façades, but in a more social setting, I found myself full of criticism of others.

In one of the exercises we did that weekend, we were asked to spend time connecting with people through our eyes alone. We weren't allowed to speak as we spent time gazing into one another's eyes. I was quite comfortable with this activity, as I had often sat with hospice patients who could only communicate in this way. Other participants really struggled with this exercise.

Soon I found myself face to face with the woman in the sexy dress whom I had so quickly judged. Gazing into her beautiful green eyes, I saw past the make-up and the sexy clothes. As we looked into each other's eyes, I felt totally connected to her. As we held our gaze on one another, her tears began to flow and I experienced an overwhelming sense of compassion for her.

She later shared with me that she had never felt truly seen until that exercise. All her life she had just wanted to be seen! I realized that this was exactly what I had wanted as well. With this awareness, I forgave myself for having judged her, realizing that my judgment had been based on my fear of not being seen in the shadow of this very striking, well-put-together woman. That day we were both seen for the beautiful souls that we are.

The weekend was powerful, but it was also far from easy. We were encouraged to look deeply at how we "showed up in the world." I entered the workshop believing that I was a kind, genuine, honest woman. But when I really started to examine my behavior, I saw that I lied frequently— I lied to others and I lied to myself. I was raised to put other people's needs before my own, and that's what I did most of the time. Wanting to be liked or loved or accepted, I told people what I thought they wanted to hear so that they would have a favorable opinion of me.

I often said "yes" when I really wanted to say "no." Later I would lie to get out of the commitments I had never intended to keep. I didn't have a strong sense of who I was or even what I wanted since I had spent so much of my life bending to please others. I entered into romantic relationships with this same lack of self-awareness. Like a chameleon, I transformed myself into whatever my partner wanted me to be. I looked to them for validation that I was lovable. With that came the inevitable resentment and anger, all of which I pushed so far down into the depths of my being that I wasn't even aware that they were there. Consequently, there was little integrity in my relationships and that impacted all aspects of my life. I avoided developing deep relationships, as I was afraid of the expectations that others might have of me. Knowing that I had trouble saying "no," it felt easier not to engage with people. That made for a lonely existence.

During the weekend workshop I also recognized that I had spent many years blaming others. I learned how vital it was for me to start taking responsibility for my actions rather than playing martyr or victim. As I put this new life strategy into practice, I found that when I took self-responsibility I got my power back. I discovered that I really didn't want to waste any time pretending to be someone that I was not.

I began to let people see me, all of me – including my imperfections, fears and insecurities. As I did this, instead of repulsing people as I had always feared I would, I was actually able to connect more genuinely with people. When I took my armor off, others became more comfortable letting me see their real selves as well. What a revelation it was to discover that it is our vulnerability that allows us to truly connect with one another.

By the end of that emotional and invigorating weekend I felt lighter and freer than I had for years. I continued to take workshops over the next year, as I knew that I would need support in changing old ways of being that were deeply embedded in my psyche. I was committed to continuing my growth. Although these workshops kept adding to the tools I needed to reclaim my power and my voice, what I would never have guessed was how big a role my patients would play in giving me the courage to follow through on my commitment to myself.

Throughout this book I have shared the compelling lessons I learned from the dying. It's one thing to intellectualize what I experienced and what my patients taught me, but none of it meant a lot to me until I started actively incorporating the insights I'd gained from my patients into my life. I didn't want to get to the end of my life and have regrets, as many of my patients had, about the things I hadn't done. Thanks to my patients I had gotten really clear on the importance of embracing life.

Gifting me through their very personal final dance, each new patient became my dance partner for a time and helped me to strengthen my commitment to living my life to the fullest. Because of them, I have learned the importance of not settling for the seduction of safety.

I have learned to take risks in order to pursue my dreams. Those risks have included my trip around the world, moving to Hawaii, singing in front of 200 people when I was terrified to sing, and writing this book. It's hard to put into words just how my world has expanded has become thanks to the treasures I have received from my patients. Applying their lessons to my life has been nothing short of miraculous!

In ways large and small, I have changed how I show up in the world as a result of my hospice work. I have been privileged to get to know courageous women who had lost their hair, their breasts, and their dignity and yet continued to shine brightly, dancing through their last days with grace, majesty, and blinding beauty. Being with them has unquestionably put things into perspective for my life. I have become less critical of my body, worrying about my weight, and feeling any stress over whether my clothes are in fashion or not. I am so grateful to those admirable women who have demonstrated so clearly for me what true beauty looks like.

The word that best sums up what I have gained from my years in hospice is "freedom." When I stopped worrying about what others thought of me it gave me a sense of freedom I had not experienced before. I found myself more at ease talking in front of groups. I stopped trying to be what I thought people wanted me to be and began valuing myself as I am. Saying "No" got easier. I relaxed more into my life. All of the newfound freedom allowed me to start incorporating more and more of the qualities that I admired in my patients and the key lessons that they shared with me out of their own life experiences.

As I continued on my hospice journey, I became ever more curious about the "unseen world." It amazes me now when I stop to think about how much my beliefs have shifted over the years. The better part of this shift has been directly connected to my ongoing work with the dying. In my early days as a hospice social worker, I was doubtful, cynical, and quick to dismiss unexplained events as wishful thinking or manifestations of someone's grief. I imagine that lots of people respond to unusual experiences much as I did for many years. I would have an experience and then talk myself right out of it. I would tell myself it was "just a coincidence."

My beliefs have shifted so drastically that I often ask myself, "How did I get clear over here?" When I first started doing hospice work, I obsessively read books on near-death experiences, hoping that the books would give me insight into what my patients were experiencing. I became fascinated by the many forms of spirituality and read books on shamanism, the spirit world, mediums, and past lives. I have attended many Christian and Catholic churches, participated in Jewish rituals, explored Native American and Hawaiian beliefs, read about Buddhism and Hinduism, had past life regressions (and am now a certified practitioner of past life regression—that's a whole other story!). I became certified as a Reiki practitioner, practice yoga and meditation and am always curious to learn more. I've jokingly professed to being a "spiritual adventurer." As I look back at the multitude of experiences I have had, I understand why my curiosity and beliefs have continued to evolve and grow.

Over the years I have had a fascination with mediums, more for the entertainment value than anything else. I never trusted that mediumship was real, convinced that mediums were people who preyed on vulnerable, grieving people in the world. Yet there I was having experiences in which I felt people's energy when their souls left their bodies. I'd also come to believe that the deceased were sending many of my bereavement clients and me signs and messages. I asked myself, "If I can have these types of experiences, then why can't there be others who are even more tuned into the spirit world than I?" With that, I let go of my judgments about mediumship.

Today I still believe that there are some so-called mediums who do prey on grief-stricken individuals. But they aren't the only ones, there are also mortuaries that try to sell bereaved family members the "best casket;" and churches that ask for donations "so that their loved one's souls can be prayed for." Yes . . . and even some hospices can be overzealous in asking for donations during the families' vulnerable time. On the whole, however, I believe most hospices, churches and mortuaries try to do what is best for the bereaved.

For many years I identified primarily with Christianity, but now I have come to see that there are many paths to the same destination. My spiritual studies have shown me the many commonalities that run throughout world religions. The broad thread of truth that runs through all these teachings is the theme of love. In this crazy world we continue to fight over the dogmatic details, but I think we're missing the real message. I believe that if we all focused on that message of love we wouldn't care what others believe. We are one world, one human family, created from the same Source.

I realize that I do have a rare perspective due to the sheer numbers of deaths I have experienced and heard about over the years. A major contributor to that perspective is the cumulative experience that that entails— so many synchronistic events, so many unusual experiences surrounding the deaths of my patients, so many "inexplicable" happenings. To me they have become commonplace, though never taken for granted. Given all that I have seen and experienced, I know that the only "logical" thing for me to do is to believe in them. To believe in the energies that cannot be seen, in the messages that defy logic, and in the signs that cannot be explained away.

Now, when I think about the question I had when I first started working in hospice, "Is there life after this life?" I realize that there is a deep knowing within me. My answer is "Yes!" There is life after this existence. Do I claim to know *what* happens after we die? No, I certainly don't. The truth is that I don't think any of us will know for sure until it's our turn. The one thing I do know for sure is that we will all get a turn.

Today I feel great freedom and power in the knowledge of the impermanence of this life. This awareness in conjunction with the lessons my patients have shared dictates how I live my life and how I show up in the world. I can personally attest to how profoundly this knowledge can be a catalyst for change, growth and expansion. My goal in writing this book has been to help more people become truly aware of the temporary nature of life so they will be less likely to waste time worrying about trivial things, and more inclined to focus and live their dreams.

Some people might argue that "of course, everyone knows that life is impermanent!" But all too many times I have heard my hospice patients tell how, not just "time," but "life itself" *had gotten away* from them. They admit to having been so wrapped up in the day-to-day grind that they missed the flow of their own lives. Others mourn the fact that they did not allow themselves to think about death while they were fully engaged in living. They viewed it as a morbid or depressing topic, and they remained completely oblivious to it as the central message of life that it is. Still others attest to the fact that it is really depressing to get to the end of life with a bucketful of regrets rather than a bucket list with every item checked off.

As I look back at what I have experienced over the years I think, "What an adventure I have been on!" How ironic that I thought I would be helping these "poor souls" as they departed this world. Instead, I have been blessed with the opportunity to be with incredible beings at a singular and most precious time in their lives. They have not only taught me tremendous lessons but, truth be told, they saved me.

Questions to Dance With...

Are there things in your life that you would like to change? Write about them.

Pick one of the areas in your life that is not ideal and write in as much detail as possible what you would like it to look like instead.

What steps could you take today to improve that area of your life? List at least five steps and identify when you plan to achieve thm.

Final Thoughts

Ignoring Death

The fear of death follows from the fear of life.
A man who lives fully is prepared to die at any time.

~ Mark Twain ~

I N THIS "AGE OF TECHNOLOGY" which intended to provide us with the tools to vastly improve communication between and among ourselves, we have ironically become more separated, divided, and estranged than ever before. We can see this lack of connection not only in the family unit but throughout the world, with so much political unrest and conflict. Intimacy has been lost in a sea of "likes," "tweets" and text messages. We no longer celebrate others by getting together with them in person. Instead, we drown them in messages sent out to hundreds or thousands of our "friends." In pursuing this lifestyle, we have given up something precious. We have forgotten the importance of *showing up* for one another in person.

I recently had a birthday and received over 100 birthday wishes on Facebook. Fortunately for me, I also had one friend who actually asked the question and found out that I didn't have any plans for celebrating my birthday. In a delightfully old-fashioned and utterly endearing way, she dropped everything and drove an hour to my home to celebrate my birthday with me. That person-to-person interaction meant the world to me. If I had to choose between spending the day with a friend or getting 100 happy birthday wishes online, I would without hesitation choose the connection with a dear friend.

In this age of electronic gadgets, even when we come together physically, there is still a disruptive barrier between us. We are hooked on looking at our phones, our laptops or our tablets. What I can tell you is this: one of our patients' most significant regrets is not spending more quality time connecting with their loved ones (and I can say with confidence that most of our older patients are not addicted to electronics the way every subsequent generation seems to have become!)

I firmly believe that if we don't make radical changes in the way we are interacting with each other, we will wind up with even more regrets than my elderly patients' experience. Even when we are together, we often aren't connecting with each other. Let me describe to you a scene that I witness frequently in hospice. A family of two, three, or more members are all sitting around the hospital bed of their loved one, each in their own little universe, reading emails, attending to their social media, texting, talking or playing games on their phones.

I have often observed that hospice patients lose interest in television as they approach the end of their lives. Their families will talk about how they used to always have the TV on, and now the families are surprised by their lack of interest in it. I believe that a partial explanation for this is that our patients are longing for intimate connection. Their lives have slowed down tremendously— they are clearly dancing to a music and a pace that we simply don't recognize from our vantage point in life. There is a unique grace to this slow and final dance, to be sure, grace that is almost unbearable and nearly impossible to attain in our typical up-tempo, busy lives. Why? It's as if our culture has trapped us in a frenzied polka that tips the scales towards the "doingness" of life. It trains us to live life as a fast dance, always in a hurry to get more things done. For most of us, it is only during the inevitable final-dance phase of life that our "beingness" gets our attention and our chronic emphasis on "doingness" falls away. In a very real sense, our lives get put into perspective – and perhaps for the first time.

During this slow-dance phase of their lives, patients long to have others get into rhythm with them, to partner with them. They want their family members to listen to their stories, to ask them questions about their lives, to take a deeper interest in them as human beings. When family members walk into the room to visit they are coming directly from their busy lives, and it is difficult for them to transition from their fast dance to the slow dance of their dying loved one. Plugged in as they are to our hectic outside world, it can be very difficult for them to slow their tempo enough to come into rhythm with their loved one. This is certainly not the case with all my families, of course. By the same token, over the last several years I have seen families struggle more and more to slow down and be truly present with their dying loved ones.

The phenomenon we are seeing today is virtually unprecedented. The baby boomers, the largest generation in the U.S., second only to the millennials, have been burying their parents and have started dying themselves. They are reflecting more on their own lives, and many have begun to prepare for their own deaths. What we are seeing in hospice is a welcome trend, but one that often does not go far enough. At first, their focus tends toward "the business end" of dying. Wills are written or revisited, final arrangements are made, and end-of-life decisions are spelled out in advanced directives. While these legal documents and details are extremely important, there are other, equally vital issues that need to be addressed.

Our patients' experiences have clearly demonstrated what these issues are. They include unresolved spiritual issues, the healing of relationships that have been broken, sharing their true feelings with loved ones, and expressing their personal beliefs about death. For many families these are not comfortable nor easy discussions to have but are essential to bringing closure to patients and their families.

Oftentimes, when a patient brings up their terminal status, their families are quick to respond by saying things like, "Don't talk like that!" encouraging their loved one to remain positive or changing the subject altogether. What I know to be true is that these family members are just too close to the situation. Emotionally they are in pain, and the fierce pain of their grief is precisely what they have had little to no experience dealing with. They cannot bear the thought of losing their loved one. I truly understand and honor the depths of their grief. Even I, a professional grief counselor, am not immune to the overwhelming nature of being confronted with the death of a loved one.

On a recent visit home at Thanksgiving, my parents sat me down and wanted to tell me about the final arrangements they have made for themselves. As the "child" of my parents, I didn't want to hear them talk about their death wishes and the arrangements they had made for after their deaths. The initial reaction from my daughter-identified-self was strong denial. I did not want to face the fact that my parents would be gone someday. And I heard the words "Don't talk like that!" come out of my mouth after their initial introduction of the sensitive topic of their deaths.

But the trained social worker within me knows this: when we stop the conversation that our parents, elderly loved ones, or dying loved ones want to have with us, we shut them down. We deprive them of the opportunity to have a discussion— albeit a potentially difficult one— that could be healing for all parties involved.

Fortunately, my hospice-worker-self won out. I caught myself and retracted my statement to my parents. Then I told them that I welcomed the discussion that was to follow, knowing how vital it was. So, yes, I do know firsthand how difficult it is to stay open for these discussions and want to encourage you to do so. I can promise that you will be glad you did.

What I really want you to understand is the very thing that took me several years to learn as a bereavement counselor. A big part of what family members often need to process after a loved one's death is that they never got to have a conversation with their loved one about their terminal status, nor did they get to talk about how they felt knowing that their loved one was dying. Ironically, what family members cannot bring themselves to talk about before their loved one dies is what causes them to grieve the most after their loved one's death!

I have come to understand that facing the reality of death can benefit everyone involved and I encourage my hospice families to push past their discomfort whenever possible. However, it's important to mention that at times denial can be a valuable coping mechanism. Sometimes people are in denial up to the last day or two, and some stay there until the end. They know instinctively that if they accept the reality of what is happening (their beloved is dying) they will not be able to function, which is vital as caregiver.

Our patients also have the right to be in denial. This became abundantly clear to me when I was a new hospice social worker and was asked by a seasoned hospice nurse to have a talk with a patient named Tracie who was "not facing reality." The nurse told me, "You need to make Tracie understand that she is terminally ill. She needs to understand what is going to happen to her." New in this position and eager to please, I agreed to have this conversation with Tracie.

During my next visit with Tracie I proceeded to give her "the cold, hard facts" (details she had not asked for about her prognosis and the disease progression — what she might experience). I was so fixated on doing what the nurse had asked me to do that I did not pick up on the nonverbal cues that Tracie was giving me as she sat with her arms crossed and her head down, politely listening. Truth be known, I was very uncomfortable with having this conversation but left feeling like I had done what I was supposed to do. Tracie said very little during our time together. I think I blindsided her with the information I dumped on her.

The next week I went back to Tracie's for our weekly visit. She was generous enough to allow me to come back into her home. As soon as I arrived we sat down and had a candid conversation. She said firmly, "Cheryl, don't ever do that to anyone again! I didn't ask for that information and I didn't want it. I didn't sleep for days after you talked to me. You need to respect where I am. I choose not to look at those things." I felt sick to my stomach as I realized what I had done to her and apologized profusely, thanking her for being so frank with me. I was humbled by this experience. And once again found myself sitting with a teacher.

I believe people do the best they can under incredibly challenging circumstances, and sometimes the best they can do is to be in denial. Often when someone is dying slowly the denial softens as they begin to decline physically, and it becomes more obvious that they are not going to have a recovery—but sometimes they just can't face it— it's just too frightening a reality. I know they will be forced to face it soon enough.

At some level, most people who are dying know when their bodies are shutting down, even if no one from the medical world has told them that that is what is happening. I believe that everyone has a right to know, because it gives them an opportunity to say goodbyes, to take care of unfinished business, and to make sure their affairs are in order. I share these things with family members who want to protect their loved one by not telling them. I have learned that pro-*active engagement* at the end of their lives is an important undertaking for many patients.

However, since my experience with Tracie, whenever I have had a team member or family member tell me "they are in denial and you need to make them face reality," I tell them that is not my call. Tracie taught me that I have to let our patients and their families take the lead in this final dance. I allow them to control the pace and guide the steps, including the information I share with them. If they are not physically or mentally able to lead, then I defer to their family.

I don't know if it is largely due to the disconnection driven by the world of electronics or a combination of many factors, but I have seen that more and more people are have difficulty relating to each other. We have become uncomfortable with being vulnerable, speaking our truth, and expressing our feelings. How and where do we now begin to heal this rift in our emotional wholeness?

Some years ago I sent a card to my father to tell him how much he meant to me. I outlined all the ways that he had positively impacted my life. When I gave him the card I could tell that he was touched by it, but he responded to it by saying, "I'm not dying yet!"

On that day, as on so many other occasions, I dropped into gratitude for my hard-won training in social work. Though my first response was to feel rebuffed by his words, my training kicked in and I was able to recognize the simple truth that my words of affection made him uncomfortable.

When did acknowledging someone become something to be reserved for special occasions, funerals or the deathbed? I think many people operate this way, assuming that the best time to express what is in our hearts will be *later* and that, somehow, we will know that time when it comes. But the reality is that our lives and those we love could end in a flash.

With this in mind, I put together a program I called *Celebrate Now: An Honoring Ceremony.* At the time I was working as a bereavement counselor for a hospice company in California. The program was based on my observation over many years that, even when families are aware that their loved one is dying, they often still wait for the "right time" to tell their loved one how they feel about them. Consequently, they often miss that opportunity.

When I put together this program it was built on the premise that we should not wait until the funeral to express our feelings for our loved ones. Instead, what if we held the "celebration of life" with that family member present? It was an opportunity not only for hospice patients' families to recognize their dying loved one, but also an opportunity for our patients to acknowledge the family they would be leaving behind.

I created this program a few years after the tragedy of the September 11th terrorist attacks, when two planes crashed into the Twin Towers and a third was also overtaken and crashed. After these horrific events there were many reports of people on those three flights who knew that they might not survive reaching out to family. They were willing to risk their lives to make these calls in spite of the gun-toting terrorists on these planes, in order to have one last opportunity to tell those they loved how much they meant to them. As I thought about this, I realized that it was just as important for our patients to be able to profess their love to their family as it was for their loved ones.

Celebrating the lives of those who are transitioning is one of the most important things we can do for our patients and for their families. When we honor individuals at the end of their lives and celebrate who they are, what they have accomplished, and how we feel about them, we are celebrating the continuum of humanity - theirs and ours - in a powerful ritual that can only open and liberate all of our hearts.

One example of the power of this honoring ceremony took place spontaneously when I was with a large family who had decided to take their loved one off of life support. As they were getting ready to disconnect the machines, I encouraged the family to gather around and tell their loved one what he had meant to them. Each family member said a few words, tears streaming down their faces. There were two teenage boys in the circle who looked quite uncomfortable with all the emotional sharing. Their gaze was locked on the ground, and their faces were scrunched closed to hide any emotion.

I assured them that they did not have to say anything if they didn't want to. One of the boys told his grandfather in a whisper how much he meant to him. The other continued to stare at the floor and said nothing, rocking back and forth looking like he might bolt out of the room at any second. After everyone had spoken what they needed and wanted to, the nurse began to unhook the patient from the life support machines. As they did, the other teenager who hadn't said anything stepped forward hurriedly and blurted out, "I love you grandpa!"

After the machines were disconnected we were surprised to see our patient breathing on his own. One of the teenagers shot me a killing glance as if to say, "I cannot believe you just put us through that!" Gratefully, one of his family members pointed out that their grandfather hadn't seen some of the people in the room, his close relatives, for several years, and suggested that "grandpa might want to hang out for a while" with all of them.

He did "hang out" with them for a few more hours. His family took that opportunity to elaborate in more detail on the difference he had made to them and continued to acknowledge him until he took his last breath. Although his grandsons might have initially been irritated with me for putting them on the spot to express their feelings, in the long run they would be glad that they had shared what was in their hearts with their beloved grandfather. Even in the face of their loss, the family united in love.

Another poignant interaction I had was with the daughter of one of my patients. She had watched me interacting with her dying father, holding his hand, leaning in to catch his every word, being fully present with him. As I was leaving the room she pulled me aside with a genuine smile on her face and said, "Thank you. I have been so unsure of how to be with my dad, and today you've shown me how."

Many people don't know what to do or say when someone is dying. It's one of the reasons family members often use electronics while sitting with their dying loved ones. The electronics simply give them a way to harness their attention and "take action" when there is really very little they can "do" to help. At their loved one's bedside they are, understandably, ill at ease. They simply don't know how to be, what to say nor how to provide comfort.

I have slowly come to understand that it is simply our "being there" that assists our patients the most: that we sit by their bedside . . . that we graciously and gratefully listen to whatever they want to say or request . . . that we are simply caring, yet dispassionate, witnesses to the culmination of their lives. Even those who have expressed lofty dreams that are impossible to fulfill have come to rest in peace in our presence. Simply because we were present.

Dear readers, please hear this. Being "fully present" to your dying loved one is the most generous gift you can give them, and it is the most beautiful gift that you can give yourselves. Understand that, as hospice workers, the greatest calling we answer to is to simply "be present" to our patients. So please know that each of you can do just that . . . you have the innate capacity and the emotional wherewithal. You *can* choose to be present to your loved ones, no matter how hard it may feel at times. In spite of how foreign it may feel – because you've never done it before and because you have no idea "how to do it" – trust me when I say — you can do it! Don't be afraid to show them that you love them. And don't wait to celebrate who they are in your life.

May you be present within in your own life. This life is a wonderful dance. You can choose to sit on the side lines, or you can relax into the rhythm of life, listen for the music, and follow your soul's lead.

Let's imagine that there has always been a symphony playing in the background of each of our lives. What I can tell you about my personal symphony is that, since I arrived at hospice, my life has been unexpectedly blessed and enriched many fold because my patients have become the guest conductors of my personal symphony. They have helped me wake up to life and to hear the beautiful score that is at the heart of my own life. Their slow-dance mode has helped me to quiet down internally enough to hear the music, and their stories have encouraged me to feel and tap into the rhapsody of life, of my life. May the stories I've shared with you inspire you to become aware of the unique symphony that is playing in the background of your life, and may it lead you to a more joyful and lyrical expression of your true self.

Questions to Dance With...

Describe a time when you have acknowledged someone or been acknowledged.

How did it feel?

Who is someone you would want to acknowledge, and what would you want to say to them?

If you were given a prognosis of six months or less to live, what would you want to accomplish? Are there relationships you would want to heal? Expand upon this.

Healing Exercises

Uisualizations and Journaling

To Support You Through Loss or Change

I am including these guided visualizations and journaling exercises for further exploration. I have used all of these visualizations with clients and/or myself when going through a loss or change that was difficult. You may find the short writing activities comforting if you are going through a challenging time.

The first visualization, *Your Legacy* can be helpful in clarifying what you want in life and if you are satisfied with your accomplishments so far.

The second and third visualizations (*Unfinished Business* and *Reminiscing)* may be especially beneficial if you have experienced the loss of someone you love through death or a break-up. Please be aware that, if your loss is recent, you may want to wait a while before diving in. Your heart may be too tender yet for some of these exercises. Please trust your instincts on this. If you facilitate bereavement groups, these visualizations can also be a powerful tool for supporting your clients in their healing journey.

After each of these visualizations there are journaling exercises to support you in further exploration and deepening the process.

The final visualization, *I've Got You* is a simple but powerful process that you can use anywhere, anytime to soothe and comfort yourself.

I have also included instructions on how to use *Gentle Awakenings* to support you through difficult times.

The tools provided in this section are intended to be supplemental to the other healing modalities you are working with. They are not meant to take the place of a counselor. If you are suffering from severe depression or other mental health issues I encourage you to seek professional help first. Wait until you have a good support system and permission in place and feel more stable before engaging in these exercises. If you are under the care of a psychiatrist or physician for mental health issues, it is important to get permission before engaging in these visualizations.

There are several different ways to work with these guided visualizations.

- You can read through the text of the visualization first and then go through the process on your own from memory.

- You may want to record yourself reading the visualization text aloud.

- You may want to ask someone dear to you to read and record the visualization for you.

- You may go to **www.cheryldeines.com** and download my recordings of these guided visualizations.

- Whatever route you choose to take, please do the visualizations only when you are in a safe, quiet place. Be sure to give yourself enough time. This is healing work that you are embarking on. Please give yourself the gifts of space and time so that ease and grace can drop in and be your partners on these journeys.

Be aware from the outset that emotion may come up as you take these journeys. Images may arise. Long-buried memories may surface. Do your best not to resist any of it. Allow yourself to feel your feelings. Allow your feelings to flow. If deep emotion comes up, know that it comes up because you are ready to acknowledge it and because it is ready to be released.

Much of the anxiety that people experience when they are grieving is a result of their efforts to hold down the very feelings that need to emerge and be expressed. If you allow yourself to really feel what you are feeling, you will no longer be held hostage by feelings of anxiety or concern that your emotions will "leak out" at inopportune times. I encourage you to be gentle and patient with yourself during this process. When emotion comes up, let it come, dear one. I promise you that when you allow yourself to feel your feelings, you absolutely **will** survive. Your feelings are the pathway to your healing.

Your Legacy

I experienced a similar visualization to the one I am sharing here when I first started on a path of self-exploration that resulted in powerful changes in my life. It helped me gain clarity on what I valued in life and what my next steps would be. May it serve you in the same way.

Get comfortable in your chair, close your eyes, and take a deep breath. As you exhale, release any tension from the day. On your next breath imagine that you're breathing in a soft white light. As you take a slow deep breath visualize a white light rising up from the base of your spine and through the top of your head. When the light gets to the top of your head, hold your breath for the count of ten. One, two, three, four, five, six, seven, hold it, eight, nine, ten, then release. Good. Now breathe normally for a few breaths. Again bring the white light up with your breath through your spine, your neck, and hold it at the top of your head (for 10 seconds) . . . hold . . . hold . . . and release. Good. Now breathe normally for a few breaths. One more time, take a deep inhalation as you see the white light slowly moving up your spine. (Hold the light at the top of your head for a count of ten.) Then release. Great! Now relax and breathe naturally...

Now see, feel, or sense yourself walking in a beautiful golden meadow. As you walk along the narrow trail notice a butterfly playfully fluttering around you and feel the sun warming your face. It is a perfect spring day with purple and yellow wild flowers growing all around. Listen to the sounds of nature, as the trail leads to an opening into a forest. Continue to follow the trail, listening to the leaves rustling in the wind, birds singing. Feeling safe and secure as you continue to walk surrounded by majestic trees, you come across a stream trickling over jagged rocks. You find the sound of the water soothing and begin to walk along the stream, going deeper and deeper into the forest. Notice little animals curiously peeking out of holes and from behind rocks. You feel content in this beautiful place.

As you continue to walk along the trail, you hear music in the distance and notice that people are gathering in a clearing up ahead. Curious, you move towards the crowd. As you get closer, you realize that you know these people. They are people from your life. You recognize people from work, friends, relatives, and there are people that you haven't seen for a long time. One by one, they are going up to a podium and sharing about the life of someone who has recently died. As you listen to what they are saying about this person, you realize they are talking about you. You are witnessing your own memorial service.

Listen as, one by one, your friends and family stand up to honor you. They share stories and talk about how much you meant to them, and how you impacted their lives. Look around and notice who is there. Who came to see you off? What kinds of things are they saying about you? What accomplishments are they talking about? What did they love about you? What stories are they telling about you?

As you listen notice how you are feeling. Are you proud of what they have to say about you? What accomplishments are they talking about? Do you have regrets? Is there something that you had hoped to accomplish that didn't happen? Is there someone who has NOT come to see you off because of something unhealed between you— someone who might be struggling with your death because of unfinished business between you? Who was proud to have known you? Who was inspired by you? Listen to what else is said about you . . .

Now, the stories have been told, goodbyes have been said, and the crowd has begun to disperse. And it is time for you to join the living, as this was just an exercise in awareness. Remember, you still have a chance to accomplish those dreams, to heal relationships, and to take care of unfinished business.

Let these images fade into the light, become aware of your body moving and stretching, taking a few deep breaths to bring yourself fully into this moment, and when you're ready open your eyes.

Journaling Exercise:

1. Take a few moments now to write about this experience. Make note of what you were most proud of, the things you regretted, and relationships that might need your attention.

2. Another powerful exercise is to write an obituary. If you were to die today, what would your obituary say? For some, this exercise may seem morbid, but there is a lot of power in reflecting on where we are in life. As you read in *The Final Dance* many people I worked with in hospice talked about how life got away from them. They weren't paying attention, and then all of a sudden it was over. I whole heartedly invite you to pay attention to your life, starting now. I have no doubt you have much more latitude than you've been giving yourself in choosing how to live your life, the risks you can take, and the things you can accomplish.

Unfinished Business

This visualization can be used to help you feel more connected with your deceased loved ones. While using this visualization in one of my grief groups, one of the bereaved members expressed tremendous gratitude. She said she had not been able to picture her husband's face since his death until we did this exercise.

Sit in a comfortable position with your eyes closed, back erect, feet flat on the floor. Your hands resting comfortably in your lap. Feel the chair supporting you. Notice your breathing. Take deep cleansing breaths in and out through the nose. Breathe in slowly for three counts, hold it briefly, and then breathe out to the count of four. Feel your body beginning to slow down. Let your whole face sag and your jaw loosen. Relax your neck and shoulders. Allow this relaxation to flow through the rest of your body, down your back and stomach, relaxing your arms and legs. Feel the energy flowing from your feet into the floor, grounding you. Know that you are safe as you begin this inward journey. Become aware of a growing relaxation and calmness.

Imagine yourself walking along a beautiful path surrounded by nature. Become aware of the sunlight warming your face, a gentle cool breeze soothing you as you listen to the song of the birds. Notice your surroundings: the trees, the wind rustling the leaves, the sweet scent of flowers as the fresh air cleanses your lungs. Feel a sense of peace in this lovely place.

As you are walking along the path you notice a bright light in the distance. As you get closer to the light you see the silhouette of a person within the light. This person is walking slowly in your direction. As they come closer, you recognize them and realize that it is one of your deceased loved ones. You continue to feel a sense of calmness, knowing you are safe through this encounter. As they draw nearer, be aware of any feelings you are having as you meet your loved one on this path. You may embrace or join hands or just connect with your eyes as you stand face to face. Take a moment to reconnect with your loved one.

Is there anything that has remained unspoken between you? If so, this is your opportunity to say it. What do you need to say to your loved one? Say it now. (Give yourself time to express yourself to him or her.)

Are there things that you would like to hear from your loved one? This is an opportunity to hear those things. What do you need to hear from your loved one? Hear it now. (Again, let your loved one fully reveal his or her message to you.)

Now take a moment to remember the ways this person impacted your life. What did you learn from them? Are there values or qualities that you possess from having them in your life? Tell your loved one how your life has been influenced because they were in it (Don't rush). Are there ways that you intend to or have honored their life? Tell them about this.

How has your life changed since they have been gone? Tell them about this. (Pause for 20 seconds.) What steps have you taken to recreate your life. Tell them.

Before saying goodbye, you agree to return to this place to meet again whenever either of you desires to do so. You embrace and say goodbye and your loved one leaves you with these parting words . . . (Hear exactly what your loved one has to say.) Before your loved one leaves they inform you that they have a gift for you. Receive the gift.

Now, feeling a sense of peace as you know you can return here any time, you watch your loved one turn and walk back down the path. Notice that everything looks a little more vibrant; your body feels lighter. Watch them merge with a ray of sunlight, and as their image fades you are left with a sense of well-being. You feel comforted by the fact that you can come back to this place at any time to connect with them. As the images fade you become aware of your body. Again take a few deep cleansing breaths, wiggle your fingers and toes. When you're ready, you can open your eyes.

Journaling Exercise: Take a few minutes to write down feelings, memories and insights that may have come up during this exercise.

Reminiscing

When a relationship ends due to death or a break up, we often can only remember the difficult times at first, or we put our loved one on a pedestal and romanticize the relationship. In order to heal we have to remember it all. May this visualization help you to reconnect with some of those memories.

Get comfortable, allow your eyes to close as your hands rest comfortably in your lap, your feet flat on the floor. Feel Mother Earth below you, supporting you, holding you as your body relaxes. Allow your body to soften into the chair. Place your focus on your breath, taking a few deep, conscious breaths into your belly and slowly exhaling. Letting go of any tension. Take another deep belly-breath in for the count of three; one, two, three. Now hold it for the count of three, one, two three, exhale slowly to the count of four-one, two, three, four; repeat this three times. Breathing in for three counts, holding for three and then exhaling for four. With each inhalation feel your lungs expand; with each exhale feel yourself relax even more-letting go. (Pause to allow them to continue breathing).

Begin to breath at your own pace. As you do so, straighten your spine to allow the energy to flow easily from the base of your spine to the top of your head. Feel your feet planted firmly on the ground, the energy of Mother Earth below your feet, grounding you. Becoming more and more relaxed, allow your breathing to be easy (silence for 15 seconds).

Now as you notice your breath filling your lungs, silently ask yourself, "Who takes in this breath?" As you release this breath ask, "Who exhales this breath into this natural cycle that began at birth and will end at the time of death?" (pause 10 seconds)

Now bring your attention to the center of your heart, placing both hands over your heart. Notice your heart beating. Listen for your heart beat. Ask yourself "Who beats this heart?" (pause 10 seconds) "Who pumps the blood in this effortless flow that began at conception and will end at the time of death?" (pause 10 seconds)

Now, as you are deeply connected with your own life force, take a moment to remember the life of a person you loved who is no longer in your life. (pause 10 seconds). See their face (pause 10 seconds). Breathe in their essence (pause 10 seconds). Remember their life (pause 30 seconds). What brought them joy? What made them laugh out loud? (pause 10 seconds) What made them sad? What made them angry? What annoyed them? (pause 10 seconds). Remember a playful time. Remember a difficult time. Remember it all (30 seconds). What made them special to you? (pause 10 seconds). Are there aspects of this person that you have incorporated into your life? (pause 10 seconds). What is your favorite memory of this person? What was their favorite color? What was their favorite food? What did you love most about them? What annoyed you? What else comes to mind when you think about this person?

Remember the laughter. Remember the tears. All are a part of their life. All are a part of your life. Now you are ready to tell their story. Take a deep healing breath — being aware of what a gift each breath is, and slowly exhaling. With the next breath become aware of your surroundings. Wiggle your fingers and toes, connect with your body, reach to the sky — stretching—and when you're ready you can open your eyes.

Journaling Exercise: Staying in this meditative state, take at least 10 minutes to journal about this experience and the memories that came up about the person you lost, before fully reengaging in life. Write these memories in as much detail as you can remember.

I've Got You

This visualization doesn't need to be scripted and/or narrated like the preceding ones because there are relatively few details involved.

First, you want to bring yourself into a meditative state. First, set a timer. It's best to start out by meditating just 5 or 10 minutes to ease yourself in. People often make meditation more complicated than it needs to be. For those of you who are new to meditation, all you have to do is sit in a comfortable position, close your eyes, and focus on your breath. If you notice your thoughts wandering, return your focus to your breath.

After setting your timer, sit in a comfortable position, close your eyes and take a few deep cleansing breaths, just following your breath as the air passes through your nostrils and fills your lungs with air. Notice your breath as it gently leaves your body. Breathing normally, continue to pay attention to your breath. Once you have gotten into a natural easy flow with your breath, wrap your arms around your body and start rocking in an easy, gentle way. Say silently to yourself. "I've got you, I've got you. I've got you."

You can imagine your mother, a spiritual teacher, a lover, an angel, or God holding you— anyone who is comforting to you. The image that comes to me is often a big-bosomed grandmother. (I think it's my grandmother Gladys.) I imagine sinking into her softness as she holds me, rocks me, and sometimes sings to me. It can be whatever or whoever brings you comfort.

When I meditate, I often visualize this image. It started out as a conscious effort on my part. Now, if I am having a hard time getting into my meditation and my thoughts are elsewhere, I will hear an internal voice say, "Come and sit with me for a while." I allow Love to hold me and rock me, and I hear a voice saying "I've got you, I've got you."

Gentle Awakenings

Here is tool that is readily available and can be used to support you through difficult times in your life.

A tool I've used during difficult times is music. Several years ago, I had quit my job to move back to California from Hawaii. I ended up getting really sick at a time when I had no health insurance. I was running out of money and started feeling really anxious about my circumstances. The anxiety was most prevalent when I awakened in the morning. So, I would set my alarm to play some of the songs on my iPhone, which I was using as my alarm clock. There were two songs I chose. Both songs were by singer-songwriter Karen Drucker, who sings positive, uplifting chants.

The song I found most comforting was called *All Is Well*. When my alarm went off in the morning, I would wake to her angelic voice singing, "All is well, all is well, you are safe and all is well." Because it was a chant, these words were repeated over and over again, entering into my subconscious before I began to wake up, and it soothed me. I also used a song called *I Am So Blessed*. When I was waking up to this song, I woke up immersed in gratitude. It was a soft way to ease into my day and reduced any anxiety or fear I was feeling. Honestly, those songs were a significant part of what got me through that time in my life. And I still find comfort in waking up to them. Of course, the songs that spoke to and comforted me may not be the same songs you would want to wake up to, but I encourage you to use try this if you are ever feeling anxious or fearful. It's a beautiful way to start your day, no matter what's going on!

Acknowledgements

To Luella and Lee Deines (my mom and dad). Mom, you taught me how be aware of other people's needs and to care for them with compassion and kindness. Dad, you modeled for me the importance of a strong work ethic, honesty, and integrity. Through your actions you have both demonstrated the importance of family, commitment, and unconditional love. Thank you for always being there for me. I am who I am because of the two of you.

To my loving family, including my grandmother Louise, my brothers Rusty, Kevin and Mark, my sisters Shelly and Karen, brothers-in-law Chuck and Dave, my sister-in-law Dori, as well as my 19 nieces and nephews and my nine great nieces, nephews, and my beloved aunts and uncles. Thank you for always loving me even if you don't always understand my beliefs and view of life.

To my incredible friends—You have cheered me on, encouraged me when I was scared, gently nudged me when I wanted to stop writing, and believed in me when I didn't believe in myself. I include Belle, Keao, Linda, Susan, Darcie, Victoria, Glen, Phil, Kevin, Jennie, Barbara, Maria, Joanne, Glenda, Jeanne, Paula, Marta, Raz, Sydney, Joseph, Carol, Maggie Mae, Mick and Tess. I am blessed to have you in my life.

To my two editors, Dale Metcalfe and Maureen "Mo" Rafael, I thank you for your generosity of time, energy, and creativity. Dale, you gave me the confidence to write as you cleaned up my first drafts with your keen eye for detail and your gentle, loving encouragement. Thank you for believing in me. Mo, thank you for working magic with my book, giving it structure and depth and taking it to the next level. You really "got" what I was trying to create and helped me to bring it into form.

And Ariana D'Arrigo for your generosity, dedication, creative flare, and the exceptional work with my interior design and the beautiful cover. It's truly a work of art.

About the Author

CHERYL DEINES WAS BORN IN a small town in Nebraska. She attended the University of Nebraska, earning a Bachelor's Degree in Social Work. She worked for the State of Nebraska for ten years with Child Protective Services. During that time she returned to school and graduated with a Master's Degree in Social Work. During her graduate program she completed an internship with hospice. Much to her surprise she fell in love with hospice work. She found that being a caring companion to people during their dying days is exquisite, sacred, and privileged work. She has worked as a bereavement counselor and a medical social worker in hospice for seventeen years.

Cheryl's intention is to live her life fully. "Settling for less" is not in her stars. She attributes her bold approach to life to the magnificent life lessons she has learned from her dying patients during her many years of hospice work.

Cheryl's singular goal in writing *The Final Dance* is to help people live their lives to the fullest. She believes that the direct application of the wisdom she gained in hospice can enhance the lives of her readers. Her hope is that it will help them "reverse-engineer" their lives so that their bucket lists will be all checked off by the time they get to the end of their lives, with no regrets in sight.

She continues to work as a hospice social worker. She also facilitates creativity and empowerment groups and is a motivational speaker who shares the profound lessons she has learned from the dying to inspire others to live more courageously.

www.cheryldeines.com

Made in the USA
San Bernardino, CA
08 January 2019